Microeconomics

Revision Guide for the Introductory Economics Student

Appropriate for the following courses:

Advanced Placement Microeconomics
International Baccalaureate Economics, Higher and Standard Level
A Level Economics
Introduction to Microeconomics at the university level

JASON WELKER

www.welkerswikinomics.com

ISBN: 1482064189
ISBN-13: 978-1482064186

DEDICATION

For Libby

CONTENTS

Introduction to the Series

Thank you for purchasing the Welker's Wikinomics Microeconomics Revision Guide. This book is just one of many resources available from Welker's Wikinomics, a website created in 2007 to provide Economics students and teachers with resources to help them learn Economics in an easy and enjoyable manner.

Jason Welker teaches International Baccalaureate and Advanced Placement Economics at Zurich International School in Switzerland, where he has lived with his wife since 2008 (and as of 2012, his new daughter). Prior to teaching in Zurich, Jason taught Economics at the Shanghai American School in China. Jason graduated from university with degrees in Economics and Education after spending his own high school years living and studying at an international school in Malaysia.

In addition to this book, Welker's Wikinomics also publishes a revision guide for Macroeconomics and International Economics appropriate for students in either the AP or IB Economics class (standard and higher level), or an introductory Macroeconomics course at the university level. The Macroeconomics revision guide includes chapters on the following topics:

- GDP and its Determinants
- Aggregate Supply and Aggregate Demand
- Unemployment
- Inflation
- Economic growth
- Income distribution
- Fiscal Policy
- Monetary Policies
- Supply-side policies
- Free trade and protectionism
- Exchange Rates
- Balance of Payments

Many more resources are available for free from Welker's Wikinomics online. These include:

- PowerPoints for Economics teachers covering every unit from an introductory course: www.welkerswikinomics.com/lecturenotes
- A blog that is regularly updated with news and analysis appropriate for introductory economics students: www.economicsinplainenglish.com
- Video lectures covering nearly every topic in both this revision guide and the Macroeconomic guide: www.econclassroom.com
- A mobile application providing access to all the resources from the above sites, available for both Android and Apple devices: www.econclassroom.conduitapps.com
- A variety of other resources to aid the Economics student and teacher in mastering the subject available at www.welkerswikinomics.com

As you use this guide to review, you will notice that at the top of each page there is a reference to a section from the Economics Classroom website. For example, in chapter 3, the top of each page says "www.EconClassroom.com – 1.2" By going to section 1.2 of the website, you will find video lessons relating to Elasticity.

These are here to remind you, the student, that most topics from this book are presented in video lectures by Jason at his website, www.econclassroom.com. This site is organized by section of the syllabus, which in turn correspond with chapters from this book. The most effective way to use this book, therefore, is in conjunction with the video lectures and other resources available online.

Chapter 1 – Introduction to Economics

Economics as a Social Science

- Explain that Economics is a social science
- Outline the social scientific method.
- Explain the process of model building in economics.
- Explain that economists must use the *ceteris paribus* assumption when developing economic models.
- Distinguish between positive and normative economics.
- Examine the assumption of rational economic decision-making

Scarcity

- Explain that scarcity exists because factors of production are finite and wants are infinite
- Explain that economics studies the ways in which resources are allocated to meet needs and wants
- Explain that the three basic economic questions that must be answered by any economic system are: "What to produce?", "How to produce?" and "For whom to produce?"

Choice and Opportunity Cost

- Explain that as a result of scarcity, choices have to be made
- Explain that when an economic choice is made, an alternative is always foregone
- Explain that a production possibilities curve (production possibilities frontier) model may be used to show the concepts of scarcity, choice, opportunity cost and a situation of unemployed resources and inefficiency.

Central Themes

- The extent to which governments should intervene in the allocation of resources
- The threat to sustainability as a result of the current patterns of resource allocation
- The extent to which the goal of economic efficiency may conflict with the goal of equity
- The distinction between economic growth and economic development

Economics is a Social Science

Economics is the *social science* that studies the interactions of humans in the commercial realm. Economists examine the way societies allocate their *scarce resources* towards *competing wants and needs* and seek to develop systems that achieve certain objectives, including:

- Growth in humans' standard of living over time
- Sustainable development
- Employment and stability

Microeconomics vs. Macroeconomics: Economics is divided into two main fields of study

Microeconomics: Studies the behaviors of individuals within an economy, including consumers and producers in the market for particular goods. Examples of microeconomic topics:

- The Automobile market in Switzerland,
- the market for movie tickets in Seattle,
- the market for airline tickets between the US and Europe,
- the market for vacations to Spain,

- the market for international school teachers.

Macroeconomics: Studies the total effect on a nation's people of all the economic activity within that nation. The four main concerns of macroeconomics are:
- total output of a nation,
- the average price level of a nation,
- the level of employment (or unemployment) in the nation and
- the distribution of income in the nation
- Examples of macroeconomic topics: Unemployment in Canada, inflation in Zimbabwe, economic growth in China, the gap between the rich and the poor in America

Microeconomics and macroeconomics can be broken down into many smaller topics. Some of them are identified below.

Microeconomics topics	Macroeconomics topics
Individual markets	National markets
the behavior of firms (companies) and consumers	Total output and income of nations
the allocation of land, labor and capital resources	Total supply and demand of the nation
Supply and demand	Taxes and government spending
The efficiency of markets	Interest rates and central banks
Product markets	Unemployment and inflation
Supply and Demand	Income distribution
Profit maximization	Economics growth and development
Utility maximization	International trade
Competition	
Market failure	

Fundamental Concepts of Economics

Whether we study micro or macro, there are some basic concepts that underlie all fields of Economics study

Scarcity:	Economics is about the allocation of scarce resources among society's various needs and wants.
Resources:	Economics is about the allocation of resources among society's various needs and wants.
Tradeoffs:	Individuals and society as whole are constantly making choices involving tradeoffs between alternatives. Whether it's what goods to consume, what goods to produce, how to produce them, and so on.
Opportunity Cost:	"The opportunity cost is the opportunity lost". In other words, every economic decision involves giving up something. NOTHING IS FREE!!

Model Building in Economics

A popular tool in the Economist's kit is the *economic model*. Just like scientists in other fields, economists use models to represent something from the real world.

A model of the solar system: Allows astronomers to illustrate in a simplified model the relationships between solar bodies.

A Circular Flow Model: Allows economists to illustrate in a simplified model the relationships between households and firms in a market economy.

Ceteris Paribus: Like in other sciences, when using economic models we must assume "all else equal". This allows us to observe how one variable in an economy will affect another, without considering all the other factors that may affect the variable in question.

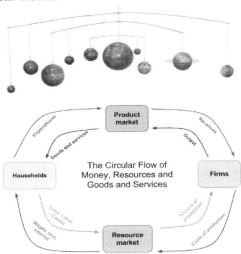

Positive and Normative Economics

Economists explore the world of facts and data, but also often draw conclusions or prescribe policies based more on interpretation or even their own opinions. It is important to distinguish at all times whether the focus of our studies is in the realm of *positive* or *normative* Economics

Positive economic statements: Each of the following statements is a statement of fact, and each can be supported by evidence based on quantifiable observations of the world.

- *Unemployment rose by 0.8 percent last quarter as 250,000 Americans lost their jobs in both the public and private sectors.*
- *Rising pork prices have led to a surge in demand for chicken across China.*
- *Increased use of public transportation reduces congestion on city streets and lowers traffic fatality rates.*

Normative economic statements: Each of the following statements is based on observable, quantifiable variables, but each includes an element of opinion

- *Unemployment rates are higher among less educated workers, therefore government should include education and job training programs as a component of benefits for the nation's unemployed.*
- *Rising pork prices harm low-income households whose incomes go primarily towards food, therefore, to slow the rise in food prices, the Chinese government should enforce a maximum price scheme on the nation's pork industry.*
- *It is the government's obligation to provide public transportation options to the nation's people to relieve the negative environmental and health effects of traffic congestion.*

Introduction to Scarcity
You may not know it yet, but you are beginning a science class. Yes, Economics is a science, and just like other sciences, it deals with a fundamental problem of nature.

- Think of Aerospace Engineering. This is a science that struggles to overcome a basic problem of nature, that of <u>GRAVITY</u>. Aerospace Engineers are scientists whose research and life's work is aimed at overcoming the problem of gravity and putting man in space.
- Economists are also scientists whose work attempts to overcome a basic problem of nature.

A riddle:
What is the basic problem of nature that the science of Economic attempts to overcome?
Hint: It arises because of the limited nature of earth's natural resources!

The answer: SCARCITY!
Scarcity is the *basic problem of Economics.*

Scarcity arises when something is both limited in quantity yet desired

Some facts about scarcity
- Not all goods are scarce, but most are
- Some goods that humans consume are infinite, such as air

Scarce (limited and desired)	Not Scarce (not limited OR not desired)
Diamonds, Apartments, Drinking water, Teachers, Doctors, Cars, Medical services	Air, Salt water, Mosquitos, Malaria, Love, HIV , Crime

So, what makes something scarce?

Here's another riddle for you…
- Nobody needs diamonds, yet they are extremely valuable
- Everybody needs water, yet they are extremely cheap

Why Are Diamonds So Expensive?
Why Is Water So Cheap?

This is known as the "diamond / water paradox". The answer lies in the fact that *economic value is derived from scarcity*

- *The more scarce an item, the more valuable it is*
- *The less scarce, the less value it has in society!*

Free Goods and Economics Goods
Goods in Economics are those things we like to consume. They are called "goods" because consuming them makes us feel good!

- Free goods are those things that we desire but that are not limited
- Economic goods are those that we desire but that ARE limited

Which of these goods are Free Goods and which are Economic Goods?					
Haircuts	Cars	Toothbrushes	Televisions	Movies	Happiness
Shoes	Vacations	Friendship	Hamburgers	Love	Jewelry
Education	Air	Fresh Water	Public Transportation	Sunshine	Rain

The Factors of Production
The production of all of the goods we desire requires scarce resources. It is the allocation of these resources between humans' competing wants that Economics focuses on.

Land	Labor	Capital	Entrepreneurship
Land resources are those things that are "gifts of nature". The soil in which we grow food, wood, minerals such as copper and tin and resources such as oil, goal, gas and uranium are scarce	Labor refers to the human resources used in the production of goods and services. Labor is the human work, both physical and intellectual, that contributes to the production of goods and services	Capital refers to the *tools and technologies* that are used to produce the goods and services we desire. Since more and better tools enhance the production of all types of goods and services, from cars to computers to education to haircuts, yet the amount of capital in the world is limited, *capital* is a scarce resource.	This refers to the innovation and creativity applied in the production of goods and services. The physical scarcity of land, labor and capital does not apply to human ingenuity, which itself is a resource that goes into the production of out economic output.

"The Basic Economic Problem"
In a world of finite resources, the wants of man are virtually infinite. The basic Economic Problem is how to allocate those limited, scarce resources between the unlimited wants of man. This problem gives rise to three questions that any and all economic systems must address. The Three Basic Economics Questions are :

1. *What should be produced?* Given the resources with which society is endowed, what combination of different goods and services should be produced?

2. *How should things be produced?* Should production use lots of labor, or should lots of capital and technology be used?
3. *Who should things be produced for?* How should the output that society produces be distributed? Should everyone keep what he or she makes, or should trade take place? Should everyone be given equal amounts of the output, or should it be every man for himself?

*** These are the three guiding questions of any Economic system***

Free Trade
The market system allocates society's scarce resources through the free, voluntary exchanges of individuals, households and firms in the free market. These exchanges are broadly known as "trade". Trade can exist between individuals, or between entire nations. Trade between countries is called **International Trade**.

Trade is one of the concepts fundamental to the field of economics.
- Voluntary exchanges between individuals and firms in resource and product markets involving the exchange of goods, services, land, labor and capital represent a type of trade.
- International trade involves the exchange of resources, goods, services and assets (both real and financial) across national boundaries.
- Trade makes everyone better off, and leads to a more efficient allocation of society's scarce resources.

Opportunity Cost
Perhaps the most fundamental concept to Economics, opportunity cost is what must be given up in order to undertake any activity or economic exchange.
- Opportunity costs are not necessarily monetary, rather when you buy something, the opportunity cost is what you *could have done* with the money you spent on that thing.
- Even non-monetary exchanges involve opportunity costs, as you may have done something different with the time you chose to spend undertaking any activity in your life.

Examples of opportunity costs
- The opportunity cost of watching TV on a weeknight is the benefit you could have gotten from studying.
- The opportunity cost of going to college is the income you could have earned by getting a job out of high school
- The opportunity cost of starting your own business in the wages you give up by working for another company
- The opportunity cost of using forest resources to build houses is the enjoyment people get from having pristine forests.

The Production Possibilities Model

- The tradeoff we face between the use of our scarce resources (or even time) can be modeled in a simple Economic graph known as the Production Possibilities Curve (the PPC). Study the graph below:

Tradeoffs in the PPC: Sarah faces two tradeoffs. She can either work or play with her limited amount of time.

- The opportunity cost of an hour of work is an hour of play
- As she goes from 3 hours of work to 7 hours of work, she gives up 4 hours of play.
- She cannot spend 10 hours working AND 10 hours playing, so Sarah has to make **CHOICES**

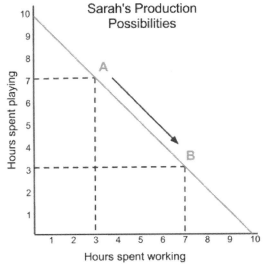

This basic model can be used to illustrate the economic challenges faced by individuals, firms, states, countries or the entire world...

Consider the hypothetical PPC for the country of Italy
This model shows that Italy can produce:

- Either 7.5 million pizzas,
- OR 750 robots
- Note, however, that Italy can NOT produce 7.5 million pizzas AND 750 robots

Italy faces a tradeoff in how to use its scarce resources of land, labor and capital. As the country moves along its PPC from point A to point D:

- It gives up more and more pizza to have more robots
- It gives up current consumption of food for production of robots, which themselves are capital goods, and therefore will assure that Italy's economy will grow into the future.

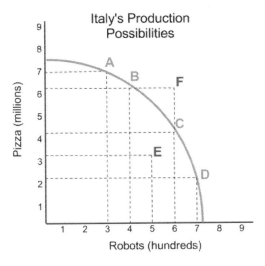

Assumptions about the PPC

- A point ON the PPC is attainable only if a nation achieves full-employment of its productive resources
- The nation's resources are fixed in quantity
- The economy is closed, i.e. does not trade with other countries
- Represents only one country's economy

Observations about points on or within the PPC
- Points ON the PPC are attainable, and desirable, since a country producing on the line is achieving full employment and efficiency
- Points inside the PPC (such as E) are attainable but undesirable, because a nation producing here has unemployment and is inefficient
- Points outside the PPC (such as F) are unattainable because they are beyond what is presently possible given the country's scarce resources. But such points are desirable because they mean more output and consumption of both goods.

Straight-line versus curved PPCs
A PPC can be either straight or bowed outwards from the origin

A straight line PPC
- Indicates that the two goods require similar resources to produce (like pizzas and calzones)
- The opportunity cost of one pizza is one calzone, so Italy always gives up the same quantity of one good no mater where it is on its PPC

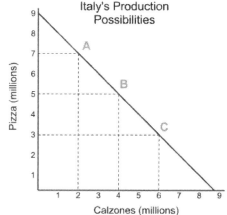

A bowed out PPC
- Indicates that the two goods require very different resources to produce (like pizzas and robots)
- As Italy increases its output of one good, the opportunity cost (in terms of the quantity of the other good that must be given up) increases.

The Law of Increasing Opportunity Cost: As the output of one good increases, the opportunity cost in terms of other goods tends to increase

Key Concepts shown by the PPC
In addition to opportunity costs and tradeoffs, the PPC can be used to illustrate several other key Economic concepts, including...
- *Scarcity:* Because of scarcity, society can only have a certain amount of output
- *Actual output:* A country's actual output is shown by where it is currently producing on or within its PPC
- *Potential output:* A point on the PPC shows the potential output of a nation at a particular time
- *Economic growth:* An increase in the quantity or the quality of a nation's resources will shift its PPC out, indicating the economy has grown
- *Economic development:* The composition of a nation's output will help determine whether the standards of living of its people are improving over time

Central Themes in Economics
Having introduced several of the topics you will study in this course we can now look at some of the major themes that will underlie all sections of the course. These include:

Key Theme #1: The role of product and resource markets in the modern economy

In the market system, there exists interdependence between all individuals.
- Households (that's us) depend on the goods and services produced by business firms, and the incomes they provide us, for our survival
- Business firms depend on households for the workers, the capital, and the land resources they need to produce the goods they hope to sell us and make profits on.

These exchanges all take place in one of two categories of market present in all market economies

Product Markets	Resource Markets
Where households buy the goods and services we desire from firms. Examples: • The market for private schools • The market for dental services • The market for airline travel • The market for football merchandise	Where business firms buy the productive resources they need to make their products: • The market for teachers • The market for dentists • The market for pilots • The market for football players

In Resource Markets:
- Households supply productive resources (land, labor, capital)
- Firms buy productive resources from households. In exchange for their productive resource, firms pay households:
  - ➤ *Wages:* payment for labor
  - ➤ *Rent:* payment for land
  - ➤ *Interest:* payment for capital
  - ➤ *Profit:* payment for entrepreneurship
- Firms seek to minimize their costs in the resource market
- Firms employ productive resources to make products, which they sell back to households in the product market

In Product Markets:
- Consumers buy *goods and services* from firms
- Households use their money incomes earned in the resource market to buy goods and services
- *Expenditures* by households become *revenues* for firms
- Firms seek to *maximize their profits*
- Households seek to *maximize their utility* (happiness)

The Circular Flow Model of the Market Economy

Market economies are characterized by a circular flow of money, resources, and products between households and firms in resource and product markets. Notice:

- Money earned by households in the resource market is spent on goods and services in the product market
- Money earned by firms in the product market is spent on resources from households in the resource market.

The incentives of Households: *Maximize Utility*
The incentive of Firms: *Maximize Profits!*

Resource Payments (Incomes for households)

In exchange for their land, labor, capital and entrepreneurship, households receive payments. The payments for the four productive resources (which are costs for firms) are...

For Land: Rent	Firms pay households **RENT**. Landowners have the option to use their land for their own use or to rent it to firms for their use. If the landowner uses his land for his own use, the opportunity cost of doing so is the rent she could have earned by providing it to a firm.
For Labor: Wages	Firms pay households **WAGES**. To employ workers, firms must pay workers money wages. If a worker is self-employed, the opportunity cost of self-employment is the wages he could have earned working for another firm.
For Capital: Interest	Firms pay households **INTEREST**. Most firms will take out loans to acquire capital equipment. The money they borrow comes mostly from households' savings. Households put their money in banks because they earn interest on it. Banks pay interest on loans, which becomes the payment to households. If a household chooses to spend its extra income rather than save it, the opportunity cost of doing so is the interest it could earn in a bank.
Entrepreneurship: Profits	Households earn **PROFIT** for their entrepreneurial skills. An entrepreneur who takes a risk by putting his creative skills to the test in the market expects to earn a normal profit for his efforts.

Key Theme #2: The Price Mechanism
Prices are how resources are allocated between competing interests in a market economy. Without tradition or command determining the allocation of resources, prices send the signals to producers and consumers regarding what should be produced, how it should be produced, and for whom.

Examples of how prices allocate resources: Imagine a city with two types of street food, hot dogs and kebabs. How would price assure that the right amount of these two foods is produced based on consumer demand?
At present,
- The price of a hot dog is $2
- The price of a kebab is $3

Due to a report on the negative effects of hot dogs on health, consumers now demand more kebabs. How will each of the two systems assure that the increased demand for kebabs is met?

Prices are signals from buyers to sellers!
As the demand for kebabs rises, they will become scarcer, causing the price to rise. Sellers will realize there are more profits in kebabs and hot dog vendors will switch to kebabs.
The price mechanism led to a reallocation of resources!

Key Theme #3: The distinction between Economic Growth and Economic Development
The emerging market economies of the world have achieved amazing economic growth for decades; but at what cost? Is increasing income and output the only thing the market system is good for?
Does getting richer assure we will be happier, live longer and healthier lives, and live in a just society? Two of the key areas of study in economics are those of growth and development. Sometimes these concepts are thought of as the same, but they are not.

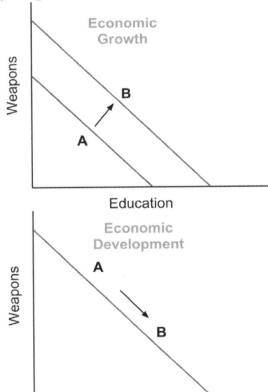

Economic Growth: This refers to the increase in the total output of goods and services by a nation over time.
- It is also sometimes defined as an increase in household income over time.
- It is purely a monetary measure of the increases in the material well being of a nation.
- On a PPC growth can be shown as an outward shift of the curve.

Economic Development: This refers to the improvement in peoples' standard of living over time.
- Measured by improvements in health, education, equality, life expectancy and so on
- Incorporate income as well, but is a much broader measure than growth
- On a PPC development can be shown by a movement towards the production of goods that improve peoples' lives

Other Key Themes in the Economics Course: Throughout the course, the following themes will be considered across all areas of our study of Economics.

- *The role of government in the economy:* In every unit of this course we will examine the appropriate role of government in the market economy. There are some who argument government should never interfere with the free functioning of markets; on the other hand, when market failures arise, the government may be needed to improve the allocation of resources.
- *Threats to sustainability of current economic trends:* What threat do global warming, environmental degradation, population growth and urbanization play to the ability of our economic systems to endure?
- *The conflict between the pursuits of efficiency and equity:* Sometimes the pursuit of wealth and economic growth leaves some individuals behind. To what extent should economic policy be concerned with income and wealth inequality? Is there a mechanism available for reducing inequality while at the same time encouraging efficiency?

Chapter 2 – Competitive Markets, Demand and Supply

Markets
- The natures of markets
- Outline the meaning of the term market

Demand
- The law of demand
- The demand curve
- The non-price determinants of demand
- Movements along and shifts of the demand curve
- Linear demand equations, demand schedules and graphs

Supply
- The law of supply
- The supply curve
- The non-price determinants of supply
- Movements along and shifts of the supply curve
- Linear supply equations and graphs

Market Equilibrium
- Equilibrium and changes to equilibrium
- Calculating and illustrating equilibrium using linear equations
- The role of prices in markets

Market Efficiency
- Consumer surplus
- Producer surplus
- Allocative Efficiency

Markets – where buyers and sellers meet
Recall from the previous chapter that *the market system* is that which most economies today are based on. Markets come in many forms, but most can be characterized as one of the following

Type	Resource Market	Product Market
What gets bought and sold?	Land, Labor, Capital and Entrepreneurship	Goods and services
Who are the demanders?	Business firms demand resources	Households
Who are the suppliers?	Households supply resources	Firms supply products made with the resources provided by households
Money flows…	From firms to households as wages, interest, rent and profits	From households to firms as expenditures (revenues for firms)
Examples	The market for: bus drivers, waitresses, bankers, janitors	The markets for: bus journeys, restaurant meals, financial services, cleaning services

Markets in the Circular Flow Model
The circular flow model shows the flow of money payments between households and firms in the market economy.

Notice:
- The interdependence of households and firms
- The motivations for individuals to participate
  - To maximize their utility or happiness for households
  - To maximize their profits for firms
- All income for households turns into revenues for firms, and vice versa.

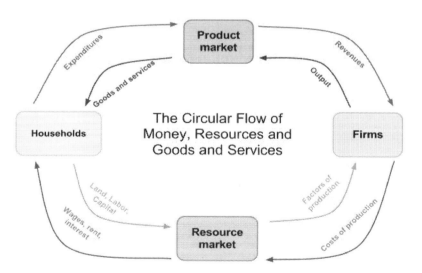

Introduction to Demand
In order for a market to function, there must be demand for a product or a resource. But what, exactly IS demand?

Determining an individual's demand :
Think of your favorite candy, and ask yourself, how much of it would you be willing to buy in ONE week if it cost the following: $5, $4, $3, $2, $1.

On the table below, write the quantity you would buy at each of the above prices in one week.

Price	Quantity
$5	
$4	
$3	
$2	
$1	

This is your weekly demand for candy.

From Individual Demand to Market Demand

Demand is defined as *the quantity of a particular good that consumers are willing and able to buy at a range of prices at a particular period of time.*

- The table you created is your individual demand for candy in one week.
- Now choose three classmates, and assume that the four of you are the ONLY consumers of candy in a particular market.
- Record all four of your demands into the table below

Price	Your quantity	Classmate 1	Classmate 2	Classmate 3	Total Demand
$5					
$4					
$3					
$2					
$1					

This is the market demand for candy in a week. The market demand is simply the sum of all the individual consumers' demands in a market

The Demand Curve

The data you recorded on your own demand and the demand of three of your classmates is in what we call *a demand schedule.* But this data can also be plotted graphically.

Drawing a demand curve:
- First draw an x and y axis

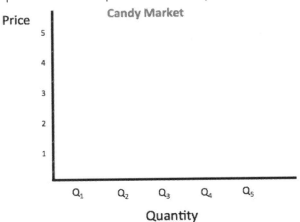

- Label the y-axis 'P' for price
- Label the x-axis 'Q' for quantity
- Include the prices from $1 to $5
- Include the appropriate quantities out to the highest total demand from your market
- Give your graph a title

Next, plot the total quantities demanded in your market at the various prices on your graph.
1. *What relationship do you observe between quantity and price?*
2. *Try to explain this relationship to your classmates*

The chances are, the points from your demand schedule formed a scatter plot, demonstrating the following:

- At higher prices, a smaller quantity of candy is demanded
- At lower prices, a greater quantity of candy is demanded

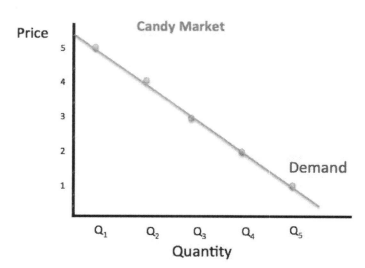

Connect the dots!
Once you have plotted the different quantities from your schedule, connect the dots, and you have *the demand curve!*

The Law of Demand:
Your demand curve should demonstrate
the law of demand, which states that *ceteris paribus (all else equal), there is an inverse relationship between a good's price and the quantity demanded by consumers*

The law of demand is a fundamental concept of market economies.
- Rational consumers will always buy more of a good they want when the price falls, and less when the price rises.
- There are three economic explanations for this phenomenon.

Explanations for the Law of Demand
- *The income effect: Real income* refers to income that is adjusted for price changes, and implies the actual buying power of a consumer. As the price of a good decreases, the quantity demanded increases because consumers now have more real income to spend. With more buying power, they sometimes choose to buy more of the *same* product.
- *The substitution effect:* As the price of a good decreases, consumers *switch* from other substitute goods to this good because its price is comparatively lower.
- *The law of diminishing marginal utility:* This law states that as we consume additional units of something, the satisfaction (*utility*) we derive for each additional unit (marginal unit) grows smaller (diminishes).

Changes in Demand vs. Changes in Quantity Demanded
Using a simple demand curve, we can show the following

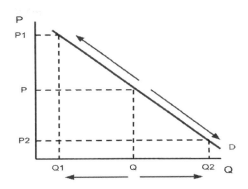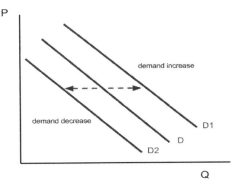

- The effect of a change in the price of a good on the quantity that consumers demand
- The effect of a change in the demand for a good

A change in price leads to a change in the quantity demanded

- As seen in the top graph, when the price of candy rises, a smaller quantity is demanded.
- When the price of candy falls, a higher quantity is demanded. *A change in price leads to a change in the quantity demanded.*

A change in demand is caused by a change in a non-price determinant.

- In the bottom graph, the entire demand curve shifts out (increases) and in (decreases)
- Shifts in demand are the result in a change in a non-price determinant of demand

To say that "demand has increased" or "demand has decreased" is to say that the entire demand for a good has shifted outwards or inwards. Such a shift is NOT caused by a change in price, rather by one of the following

The non-Price Determinants of Demand (Demand shifters)	
Tastes	A change in consumers' tastes and preferences
Other related goods' prices	A change in the price of substitutes and complementary goods
Expectations	The expectations among consumers of the future prices of a good or their future incomes.
Incomes	A change in consumers' incomes
Size of the market	A change in the number of consumers
Special circumstances	Changes in factors such as weather, natural disasters, scientific studies, etc.…

The "demand shifters" are those things that can cause the entire demand curve to move in or out. Consider the market for ice cream.

Tastes: If health conscious consumers begin demanding healthier desserts, demand for ice cream may shift to D2

Other related goods' prices:
- If the price of a complementary good, ice cream cones, rises, demand will shift to D2. There is an *inverse relationship* between the price of complements and demand.
- If the price of a substitute good, frozen yogurt, rises, demand will shift to D1. There is a *direct relationship* between the price of substitutes and demand

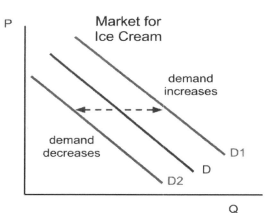

Expectations of consumers: If there is a dairy shortage expected, demand will shift to D1 (due to higher expected prices). If there is a surplus of ice cream expected, demand will shift to D2 (due to lower expected prices)

Incomes: Normal vs. Inferior goods
- If the ice cream in question is a *normal good*, then an increase in consumers' income will shift demand to D1.
- If ice cream is an *inferior good*, then an increase in consumers' income will shift demand to D2. *Inferior goods demonstrate an inverse relationship between income and demand.*

Size of the market: If the population in the town where the ice cream is sold increases, demand shifts to D1

Special circumstances: If there is a heat wave, demand shifts to D1, if the weather is unusually cold, demand will decrease to D2

Linear Demand Equations
Demand, which we have now seen expressed in both a schedule and as a curve on a diagram, can also be expressed mathematically as an equation. We will examine linear demand equations, which are simple formulas that tell us the quantity demanded for a good as a function of the good's price and non-price determinants.

A typical demand equation will be in the form: $Qd=a-bP$

Where:
- 'Qd' = the quantity demanded for a particular good
- 'a' = the quantity demanded at a price of zero. This is the 'q-intercept' of demand, or where the demand curve crosses the Q-axis
- 'b' = the amount by which quantity will change as price changes, and
- 'P' = the price of the good

Consider the demand for bread in a small village, which can be represented by the following equation:

$$Qd=600-50P$$

What do we know about the demand for bread from this function? We know that:
- If bread were free (e.g. if the price = 0), 600 loaves of bread would be demanded. Plug zero into the equation to prove that Qd=600

- For every $1 increase in the price of bread above zero, 50 fewer loaves will be demanded. Plug the following prices into the equation to prove this:

  $1 - $Qd=600-50(1)=550$
  $2 - $Qd=600-50(2)=500$
  $3 - $Qd=600-50(3)=450$
  $4 - $Qd=600-50(4)=400$

- We can also calculate the price at which the quantity demanded will equal zero. This is known as *the P-intercept* (because it's where the demand curve crosses the P-axis. To prove this, set Q equal to zero and solve for P. $0=600-50(P)$. $P=12$

The Demand Schedule
A demand equation can be plotted in both a demand schedule and as a demand curve. In the market for bread, we already determined the following:

- At a price of $0, the quantity demanded is 600 loaves. *This is the q-intercept*
- At a price of $12, the quantity demanded is 0 loaves. *This is the p-intercept*

With these numbers, we can create a demand schedule: $Qd=600-50P$

Price per loaf	Quantity of loaves demanded
0	600
2	500
4	400
6	300
8	200
10	100
12	0

Notice that for every $2 increase in the price, the quantity demanded falls by 100 loaves. This corresponds with our 'b' variable of 50, which tells us how responsive consumers are to price changes. For every $1 increase in price, 50 fewer loaves are demanded

The Demand Curve
The data from our demand schedule can easily be plotted on a graph. OR, we could have just plotted the two points of demand we knew before creating the demand schedule.

- The Q-intercept of *600 loaves*, and
- The P-intercept of $12

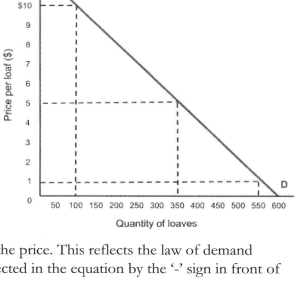

Notice the following:
- The demand for bread is inversely related to the price. This reflects the law of demand
- The slope of the curve is negative, this is reflected in the equation by the '-' sign in front of the 'b' variable.
- For every $1 increase in price, Qd decreases by 50 loaves.
- 50 is NOT the slope of demand, however, rather, it is the 'run over rise'. In other words, the 'b' variable tells us the change in quantity resulting from a particular change in price.

Linear Demand Equations – changes in the 'a' variable
As we learned earlier, a change in price causes a change in the quantity demanded. This relationship can clearly be seen in the graph.
- But what could cause a *shift* in the demand curve?
- And how does this affect the demand equation?

A change in a non-price determinant of demand will change the 'a' variable.
- Assume the price of rice, a substitute for bread, falls.
- Demand for bread will decrease and the demand curve will shift.
- *In the demand equation, this causes the 'a' variable to decrease.* Assume the new equation is: *Qd=500-50P*

Now less bread will be demanded at every price. The new Q-intercept is only 500 loaves. The demand curve will shift to the left

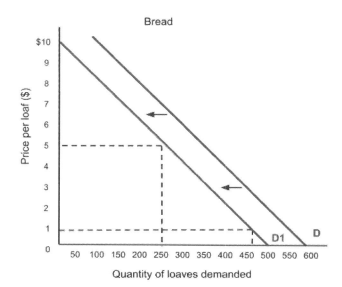

Notice the following:
- At each price, 100 fewer loaves are now demanded. In the original graph, 350 loaves were demanded at $5, now only 250 are demanded.
- Demand has decreased because a non-

price determinant of demand changed (the price of a substitute decreased, so consumers switched to rice).
- The 'b' variable did not change, so the slope of the demand curve remained the same.
- The P-intercept decreased to $10. Now, at a price of $10, no bread is demanded, whereas before consumers would buy bread up to $12.

Linear Demand Equations – changes in the 'b' variable
The 'b' variable in the demand equation is an indicator of the responsiveness of consumers to price changes.
- If something causes consumers to be *more responsive* to price changes, the 'b' variable will increase
- If something causes consumers to be *less responsive* to price changes, the 'b' variable will decrease

Assume several bakeries have shut down in the village and only one remains. Consumers now have less choice and must buy their bread form that bakery, therefore they become less responsive to price changes. The 'b' variable in the equation will decrease to 30

$$Qd=600-30P$$

Now, for every $1 increase in price, consumers will demand 30 fewer loaves, instead of 50. The Q-intercept will remain the same (600) but the demand curve will be steeper, indicating consumers are less responsive to price changes

Notice the following:
- Consumers are less responsive to price changes now.
- As the price rises from $0 to $5 per loaf, now consumers will still demand 450 loaves, whereas in the original graph they would have only demanded 350 loaves.
- Demand for bread has *increased* because there are fewer substitutes in this village.
- The new P-intercept is not visible on the graph, but it can easily be calculated. Set Q to zero and solve for P
$$0=600-30P$$
$$P=20$$

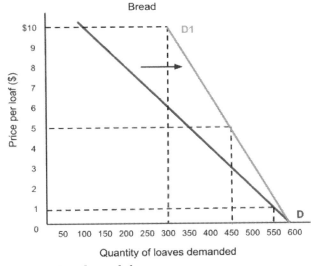

Now, at a price of $20, zero loaves will be demanded

Introduction to Supply
All markets include *buyers* and *sellers*. The buyers in a market demand the product, but the sellers supply it.

Definition of Supply: a schedule or curve showing how much of a product producers will supply at each of a range of possible prices during a specific time period.
- Different producers have different costs of production.

- Some firms are more efficient than other thus can produce their products at a lower marginal cost.
- Firms with lower costs are willing to sell their products at a lower price.
- However, as the price of a good rises, firms are willing and able to produce and sell a greater quantity of their good in the market, as it becomes easier to cover the increasing marginal costs of production. This helps to explain…

The Law of Supply
Ceteris paribus, there exists a direct relationship between price of a product and quantity supplied. As the price of a good increase, firms will increase their output of the good. As price decreases, firms will decrease their output of the good.

Whereas demand shows an *inverse relationship with price,* supply shows a *direct relationship with price.*

Consider the market for candy again.
- *An increase in the price of candy* results in more candy being produced, as more firms can cover their costs and existing firms increase output.
- *A fall in the price of candy* results in the quantity supplied falling, as fewer firms can cover their costs, they will cut back production.
- Only the most efficient firms will produce candy at low prices, but at higher prices more firms enter the market

On the graph, draw a line that illustrates the relationship between price and quantity supplied described above

The Supply Curve
The supply curve slopes upward, reflecting the law of supply, indicating that
- At lower prices, a lower quantity is supplied, and
- At higher prices, firms wish to supply more candy

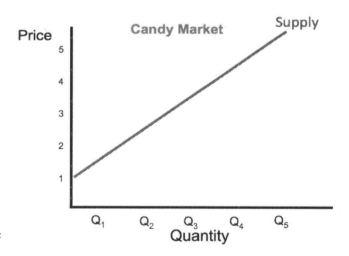

Notice that:
- The supply curve intersects the price-axis around $1. This is because no firm would be able to make a profit selling candy for less than $1. The P-intercept of supply will *almost always* be greater than zero.
- You cannot see where the supply curve crosses the Q-axis. This is because below $1, there is no candy supplied. The Q-intercept would, in fact, be negative.

The non-Price Determinants of Supply
A change in price will lead to a change in the quantity demanded. But a change in a non-price determinant of supply will shift the supply curve and cause more or less output to be supplied at EACH PRICE.

The non-Price Determinants of Supply (Supply shifters)		
S	Subsidies and Taxes	**Subsidies**: government payment to producers for each unit produce, will increase supply. **Taxes:** Payments from firms to the government, will decrease supply.
T	Technology	New technologies make production more efficient and increase supply.
O	Other related goods' prices	Substitutes in production. If another good that a firm *could* produce rises in price, firms will produce more of it and less of what they used to produce.
R	Resource costs	If the cost of inputs falls, supply will increase. If input costs rise, supply decreases.
E	Expectations of producers	If firms expect the prices of their goods to rise, they will increase production now. If they expect prices to fall, they will reduce supply now.
S	Size of the market	If the number of firms in the market increases, supply increases. Vice versa.

Changes in Supply vs. Changes in Quantity
A change in the price of good causes the quantity supplied to change. This is different than a change in supply, which is caused by a change in a non-price determinant of supply

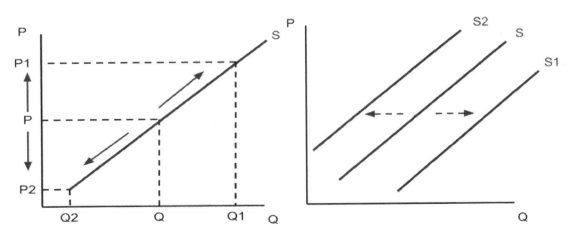

A change in price: Can be seen in the graph on the left
- Firms already in the market will wish to increase their output to earn the higher profits made possible by the higher price.
- If price falls, firms will scale back production to maintain profits or reduce losses.

A change in supply: Can be seen in the graph on the right
- If resources costs decrease, a subsidy is granted, or if the number of firms increase, supply increases to S1
- If resource costs rise, if a tax is levied, or if the price of a similar good, which firms can produce, rises, supply decreases to S2.

Linear Supply Equations
Supply can also be expressed mathematically as an equation. We will examine linear supply equations, which are simple formulas that tell us the quantity supplied of a good as a function of the good's price and non-price determinants.

A typical supply equation will be in the form:

$$Qs = c + dP$$

Where:
- 'Qs' = the quantity supplied for a particular good
- 'c' = the quantity supplied at a price of zero. This is the 'q-intercept' of supply, or where the supply curve would cross the Q-axis
- 'd' = the amount by which quantity will change as price changes, and
- 'P' = the price of the good

Consider the supply for bread in the same small village as in our demand analysis, which can be represented by the following equation:

$$Qs = -200 + 150P$$

What do we know about the supply of bread from this function? We know that:
- If bread were free (e.g. if the price = 0), -200 loaves of bread would be demanded. *Plug zero into the equation to prove that Qs=-200 at a price of zero.* Of course, -200 cannot be supplied, so if P=0, no bread will be produced.
- For every $1 increase in the price of bread above zero, 150 additional loaves will be supplied. Plug the following prices into the equation to prove this:
  - $1 - *Qd=-200+150(1)=-50*
  - $2 - *Qd=-200+150(2)=100*
  - $3 - *Qd=-200+150(3)=250*
  - $4 - *Qd=-200+150(4)=400*
- We can also calculate the price at which the supply curve will begin. This is known as **the P-intercept** (because it's where the supply curve crosses the P-axis. To find this, set Q equal to zero and solve for P. *0=-200+150(P). P=1.33*

The Supply Schedule
A supply equation can be plotted in both a supply schedule and as a supply curve. In the market for bread, we already determined the following:
- At a price of $0, the quantity demanded is -200 loaves. *This is the q-intercept*
- At a price of $1.33, the quantity supplied is 0 loaves. *This is the p-intercept*

With these numbers, we can create a supply schedule for the equation *Qs = -200 + 150P*

Price of bread	Quantity of loaves supplied
0	-200
2	100
4	400
6	700
8	1000
10	1300

Notice that as the price of bread rises from $0 to $10, the market goes from having no bread to having 1300 produced by firms.

For every $1 increase in price, quantity supplied increases by 150 loaves; this corresponds with the 'd' variable, which is an indicator of the responsiveness of producers to price changes.

The Supply Curve
The data from our supply schedule can easily be plotted on a graph. All we need is two points from the schedule to plot our curve. The following supply curve is for the equation $Qs = -200 + 150P$

Notice the following:
- The Q-intercept is not visible on our graph, since the Q-axis only goes to the origin
- The P-intercept is labeled at $1.33. This indicates that until the price of bread is $1.33 per loaf, no firms will be willing to make bread.
- The steepness of the curve is affected by the 'd' variable, which tells us that for every $1 increase in price, quantity rises by 150 loaves of bread. 'd' is the change in quantity over the change in price.

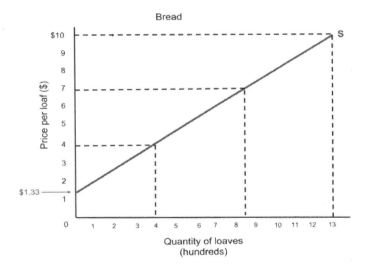

Linear Supply Equations – changes in the 'c' variable
As we learned earlier, a change in price causes a change in the quantity supplied. This relationship can clearly be seen in the graph.
- But what could cause a *shift* in the supply curve?
- And how does this affect the supply equation?

A change in a non-price determinant of supply will change the 'c' variable.
- Assume the price of wheat, a key ingredient in bread, falls.
- Supply of bread will increase and the supply curve will shift outward.

- In the supply equation, this causes the 'c' variable to increase. Assume the new equation is:

$$Qs=-100+150P$$

Now more bread will be supplied at every price. The new Q-intercept is -100 loaves. The supply curve will shift to the right

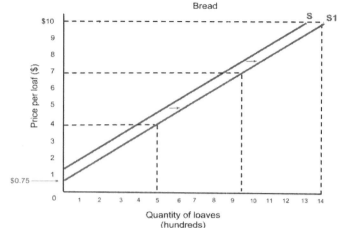

Notice the following:
- At each price, 100 more loaves are now supplied. In the original graph, 400 loaves were supplied at $4, now 500 are supplied.
- Supply has increased because a non-price determinant of supply changed (the price of an input decreased, so firms made more bread).
- The 'd' variable did not change, so the slope of the supply curve remained the same.
- The P-intercept decreased to $0.75.
  Now, firms are willing to start baking bread at a price of just $0.75, whereas before they would not begin making bread until the price reached $1.33.

Linear Supply Equations – changes in the 'd' variable
The 'd' variable in the supply equation is an indicator of the responsiveness of producers to price changes.
- If something causes producers to be *more responsive* to price changes, the 'd' variable will increase
- If something causes producers to be *less responsive* to price changes, the 'd' variable will decrease

Assume a new oven technology is developed that allows bakers to more quickly and efficiently increase their production of bread to satisfy rising demand from consumers. The 'd' variable in the supply equation increases as a result. The new equation is.

$$Qs=-200+200P$$

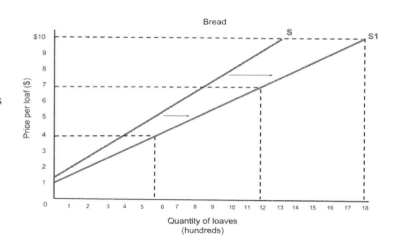

Now, for every $1 increase in price, producers will supply 200 more loaves, instead of 150. The Q-intercept will remain the same (-200) but the supply curve will be flatter, indicating producers are more responsive to price changes

Notice the following:
- Producers are more responsive to price changes now
- As the price rises from $0 to $4 per loaf, now producers will supply 600 loaves, whereas in the original graph they would have only supplied 400 loaves.
- Supply for bread has *increased* because bakers have acquired better technology.
- The new P-intercept at a lower price. It can be calculated by setting the Q to zero.

$$0 = -200 + 200P$$
$$P = 1$$

Now, at a price of $1, firms will begin selling bread, whereas before the new oven technology, a price of $1.33 was required

Market Equilibrium

We have now examined several concepts fundamental in understanding how markets work, including:
- Demand, the law of demand, and linear demand equations
- Supply, the law of supply and linear supply equations

The next step is to put supply and demand together to get…

Market Equilibrium: A market is in equilibrium when the price and quantity are at a level at which supply equals demand. The quantity that consumers demand is exactly equal to the quantity that producers supply.

In equilibrium, a market creates no shortages or surpluses, rather, the market "clears". Every unit of output that is produced is also consumed.

Equilibrium Price (Pe): *The price of a good at which the quantity supplied is equal to the quantity demanded*

Equilibrium Quantity (Qe): *The quantity of output in at which supply equals demand.*

Consider the market for bread.
- If the price were anything greater than Pe, firms would wish to supply more bread, but consumers would demand less. The market would be out of equilibrium.
- If the price were anything less that Pe, consumers would demand more but firms would make less. The market would be out of equilibrium.
- Only at Pe does the quantity supplied *equal* the quantity demanded. This is the equilibrium

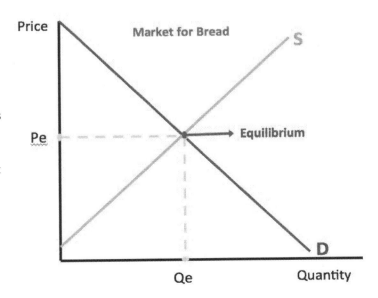

point in the market for bread.

Market Equilibrium and Disequilibrium
What if the price were NOT Pe in the market for bread?

At a price of $3
- Firms will make 12 loaves of bread
- Consumers will demand 8 loaves
- There will be a surplus of 4 loaves
- *The price must fall to eliminate this surplus!*

At a price of $1
- Firms will make 8 loaves of bread
- Consumers will demand 12 loaves
- There will be a shortage of 4 loaves
- The price must rise to eliminate this shortage!

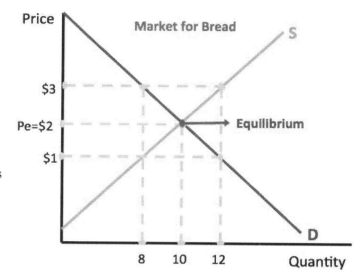

Only at Pe does this market clear, at any other price the market is in disequilibrium!

Market Equilibrium and Efficiency

When a market is in equilibrium, resources are *efficiently allocated*. To understand what this means, we must think about demand and supply in a new way.

- *Demand = Marginal Social Benefit (MSB):* The demand for any good represents the benefits that society derives from the consumption of that good. Marginal benefits decrease at higher levels of output because additional units of a good bring benefits to fewer and fewer people the more of the good exists.
- *Supply = Marginal Social Cost (MSC):* The supply of a good represents the cost to society of producing the good. For almost all goods, the greater the amount is produced, the more it costs to produce additional units of it. Think of oil. As the world produces more and more oil, it becomes increasingly harder to produce, thus the marginal cost (the cost for each additional barrel) continuously rises.

Only when the MSB = MSC is society producing the right amount of any good. If output occurs at any other level, we must say that resources are misallocated towards the good.

Once again, consider the market for bread below.

At an output of 8 loaves:
- The value society places on the 8th loaf of bread is $3, yet the cost to produce the 8th loaf was only $1.
- MSB>MSC, resources are under-allocated towards bread and *more should be produced.*

At an output of 12 loaves:
- The cost of producing the 12th loaf was $3, yet the value society places on the 12th loaf is only $1.
- MSC>MSB, resources are over-allocated towards bread and *less should be produced.*

Only at 10 loaves do the consumers of bread place the same value on it as was imposed on the producers of bread. This is the allocatively efficient level of output!

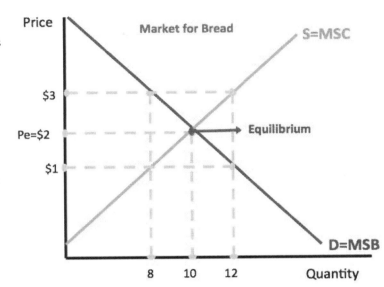

Allocative Efficiency
Allocative efficiency is achieved in a market when the quantity is produced at which the benefit society derives from the last unit is equal to the cost imposed on society to produce the last unit.

Allocative efficiency is achieved when Marginal Social Benefit = Marginal Social Cost

Assuming there are no "external" costs or benefits from the production or consumption of a good, a free market will achieve allocative efficiency when the equilibrium price and quantity prevail.

Market Equilibrium – Consumer and Producer Surplus
- *Consumer Surplus:* Consumer surplus refers to the benefit enjoyed by consumers who were willing to pay a higher price than they had to for a good.
- *Producer Surplus:* This is the benefit enjoyed by producers who would have been willing to sell their product at a lower price than they were able to.
- *Total Welfare:* The sum of consumer and producer surplus. Total welfare is maximized when a market it in equilibrium. Any other price/quantity combination will reduce the sum of consumer and producer surplus and lead to a loss of total welfare.

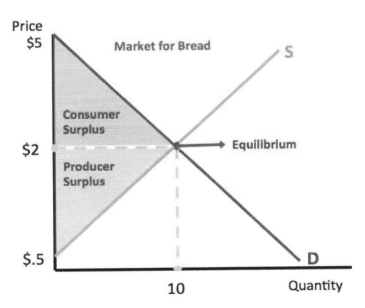

Graphically, we can identify the areas representing consumer and producer surplus, which together represent total societal welfare, as following areas.

Consumer Surplus: The area on the market graph below the demand curve and above the equilibrium price. *(10×(5-2))/2=15*

Producer Surplus: The area above the supply curve and below the equilibrium price. *(10×(2-0.5))/2=7.5*

Total welfare: The sum of the two areas. 15+7.5=22.5. $22.5 represents the total welfare of producers and consumer s in the bread market. At any price other than $2, welfare would be less than $22.5

Market Equilibrium in Linear Demand and Supply Equations
Equilibrium is a concept that can be transferred to our analysis of linear demand and supply equations just as easily as it can be applied to graphs. Assume we have a market for bread in which demand and supply are represented by the equations:

$$Qd=600-50P \text{ and } Qs=-200+150P$$

Equilibrium price and quantity occur when demand equals supply. So to calculate the equilibrium using these equations, we must set the two equal to each other and solve for price

$$600-50P=-200+150P$$
$$800=200P$$
$$P=\$4$$

Next, to find the equilibrium quantity, we must simply put the $4 price into either the demand or supply equation (since they will both yield the same quantity

$$Qd=600-50(4)$$
$$Qd=400$$

The equilibrium price of bread is $4 and the equilibrium quantity is 400 loaves

If we plot the demand and supply curves on the same axis, the intersection of the two curves should confirm our calculations of equilibrium price and quantity.

Notice:
- If the price were anything other than $4, the quantities demanded and supplied would not be equal.
- If the quantity were anything other than 400, the marginal social benefit (demand) and marginal social cost (supply) would not be equal.

$4 is the market clearing price and 400 is the allocatively efficient level of output.

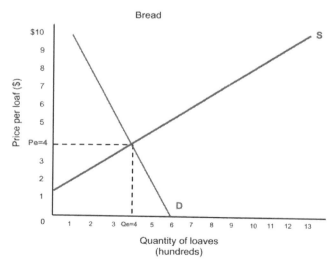

Changes to market equilibrium

Assume the cost of producing bread rises (perhaps wages for bakers have increased). The supply of bread will decrease and the supply equation changes to:

$$Qs=-400+150P$$

Assume demand remains at $Qd=600-50P$. What will the decrease in supply do to the market equilibrium price and quantity? We can calculate the new equilibrium easily:

$$600-50P=-400+150P$$
$$1000=200P$$
$$P=5$$

The decrease in supply made bread scarcer and caused the price to rise. The quantity should decrease, which we can confirm by solving for Q.

$$Qd=600-50(5)$$
$$Qd=350$$

A decrease in supply caused the equilibrium price to rise and the quantity to decrease in the market for bread!

As the supply decreases, the price of bread must rise, or else there will be shortages (as seen in the first graph). Once the market adjusts to its new equilibrium, the shortages are eliminated and the Qd once again equals the Qs (as seen in the second graph).

$$Qs=-400+150P \text{ and } Qd=600-50P$$

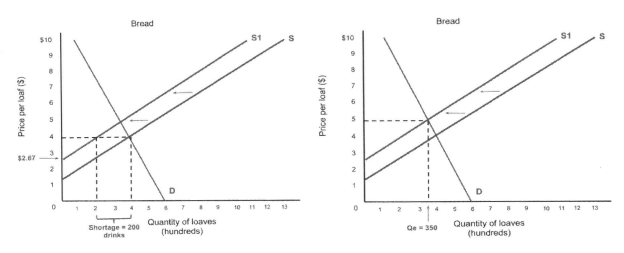

What if the demand changes? Assume consumers become less responsive to change in the price of bread and the demand equation changes to

$$Qd=400-25P$$
Supply remains the same at $Qs=-200+150P$

If we go graph these two equations, we can see the new equilibrium price and quantity
- Demand has decreased and become steeper, indicating that consumers are less responsive to price changes, yet consumer a smaller quantity overall.
- The equilibrium price is lower ($3.43 instead of $4) and the quantity is lower (314 instead of 400)

Whenever either demand or supply changes, the market equilibrium will adjust to a new market clearing price and quantity!

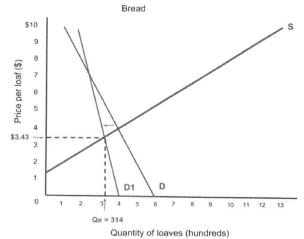

Chapter 3 – Elasticities
Price Elasticity of Demand (PED)
- PED and its determinants
- The total revenue test of PED
- Applications of PED

Cross Price Elasticity of Demand (XED)
- XED and its determinants
- Applications of XED

Income Elasticity of Demand (YED)
- YED and its determinants
- Applications of YED

Price Elasticity of Supply (PES)
- PES and its determinants
- Applications of PES

Introduction to Elasticities

Elasticity is an economic concept that refers to the responsiveness among consumers or producers to a change in a variable that affects either the market demand or the market supply. There are four types of elasticity that we will study in this unit:
- Price Elasticity of Demand (PED): Measures the responsiveness of consumers of a particular good to a change in the good's price.
- Cross-price elasticity of Demand (XED): Measures the responsiveness of consumers of one good to a change in the price of a related good (either a substitute or a complement).
- Income Elasticity of Demand (YED): Measures the responsiveness of consumers of a particular good to a change in their income.
- Price elasticity of Supply (PES): Measures the responsiveness of producers of a particular good to a change in the price of that good.

Price Elasticity of Demand – definition and formula

Price Elasticity of Demand (PED) is a measurement of *how much the quantity demanded for a good will change as a result of a particular change in the good's price.* PED can range from a value of 0 to infinity, and is calculated using the following formula:

PED=(The percentage change in the quantity of a good demanded)/(The percentage change in the price of the good)
or…

$$(\%\Delta Qd)/(\%\Delta P)$$

If, for example, we know that an increase in the price of bananas from \$4 to \$6 caused the quantity demanded to fall from 1,000 bananas to 800 bananas, we can calculate the PED for bananas.

$$\%\Delta Qd=(800-1000)/1000=-0.2\times100 = -20\%$$

$$\%\Delta P=(6-4)/4=0.5\times100 = 50\%$$

$$PED=(-20)/50 = -0.4$$

Notice that our PED has a negative value.
- This reflects the *law of demand*
- Whichever direction the price of good moves in, the quantity will always move in the other direction
- Since PED will *always be negative*, we can refer to it in its absolute value. So, the PED for bananas is 0.4

Interpretation of the PED coefficient:	
If PED is less than 1:	We say demand is *inelastic*. This means that the percentage change in the quantity is less than the percentage change in the price.
If PED is greater than 1	We say that demand is *elastic*. The percentage change in the quantity is greater than the percentage change in the price.
If PED=0:	Demand is *perfectly inelastic*. There was no change in quantity resulting from the price change.
If PED=1:	Demand is *unit elastic*. The percentage change in the quantity was identical to the percentage change in the price.
If PED = infinity:	Demand is *perfectly elastic*. The smallest increase in price causes the quantity demanded to fall to ZERO.

Interpretation of PED
Demand for bananas was 0.4. Based on our interpretations of PED from the table above, we know that demand for bananas is *inelastic*.
- For every 1% increase in the price of bananas between $4 and $6, the quantity demanded fell by 0.4%.
- Since price increased by a total of 50%, the quantity fell by a total of just 20%.
- Consumers are *relatively unresponsive to the price of bananas*.

The Determinants of PED

Whether demand for a good at a particular price is elastic or inelastic depends on several characteristics of the good itself. Just how much will consumers respond to a price change for the good? The following table presents some of the primary determinants of PED

S	Substitutes	The number of substitutes available. The more substitutes, more elastic demand, as consumers can replace a good whose price has gone up with one of its now relatively cheaper substitutes.
P	Proportion of income	The proportion of income the purchase of a good represents. If a good represent a higher proportion of a consumer's income, his demand tends to be more elastic.
L	Luxury or necessity?	Luxury or necessity? If a good is a necessity, changes in price tend not to affect quantity demand, i.e. demand is inelastic. If it's a luxury that a consumer can go without, consumers tend to be more responsive.
A	Addictive?	If a product is addictive or habit forming, demand tends to be inelastic.
T	Time	The amount of time a consumer has to respond to the price change. If prices remain high over a longer period of time, consumers can find substitutes or learn to live without, so demand is more elastic over time.

Applications of PED

The PED formula is useful for more than just telling us how much consumers respond to price changes. It can be very useful to businesses and government decision-making.

Applications of PED for	
Businesses	Businesses benefit from knowing how responsive their consumers are to price changes at any given time. • If a seller knows demand is HIGHLY elastic, he may wish to lower the price and capture many new customers. • If a seller knows demand is highly inelastic, he may wish to raise his price as he will not lose many sellers but will enjoy higher revenues.
Government	The government needs to know how consumers will respond to taxes imposed on particular goods. For example, if the government wishes to raise revenues from taxing goods, it should know that: • A tax on restaurant meals (relatively elastic) will not raise much revenue because people will just stop going to restaurants. • A tax on cigarettes (relatively inelastic) will raise lots of revenue because most people will continue smoking and thus have to pay the tax.

The Total Revenue Test of PED

A quick way to determine whether a demand is elastic or inelastic is to consider whether the revenues of sellers rise or fall as a result of a price change.

Consider the good whose demand is shown here the prices shown. (Total Revenue=Price x Quantity)

- *At $10: TR=10×0=0*
- *At $8: TR=8×10=80*
- *At $6: TR=6×20=120*
- *At $4: TR=4×30=120*
- *At $2: TR=2×40=80*
- *At $0: TR=0×50=0*

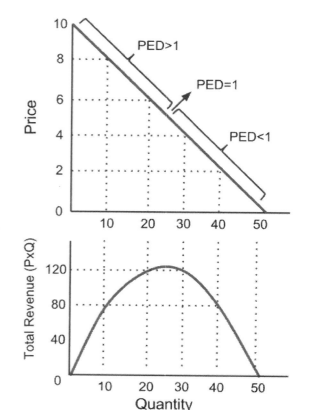

The Total Revenue Test of Elasticity:

- *If a decrease in price causes TR to rise, demand is elastic.*
- *If a decrease in price causes TR to fall, demand is inelastic*
- *If an increase in price causes TR to rise, demand is inelastic*
- *If an increase in price causes TR to fall, demand is elastic*

PED and the slope of the Demand Curve
PED and slope are different concepts.

- Slope of a line measures the rise over the run, or in the demand curve the change in price over the change in quantity.
- PED measures the *percentage change in quantity over the percentage change in price.*
- *However, by comparing the relative slopes of demand curves plotted on the same axis, we can determine the relative elasticity of different goods.*

Cross Price Elasticity of Demand (XED)

Another type of elasticity measures the responsiveness of consumers of one good to a change in the price of a related good.

For Example: Consider apples and pears, two fruits that are close substitutes for one another.

- *How will demand for pears be affected by an increase in the price of apples?*
- *XED tells us the percentage by which quantity of pears demanded will change following a particular percentage change in the price of apples.*

XED=(Percentage change in the quantity of Good A)/(Percentage change in the price of Good B) or..

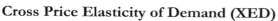

$$(\%\Delta Q \text{ of good A})/(\%\Delta \text{Price of good B})$$

Assume the following:

- Apples go from $2 to $2.50
    P1=$2, P2=$2.50

- The quantity of pears demanded rises from 30 to 50
  - Q1=30, Q2=50

XED of apples and pears =(50-30)/30÷(2.5-2)/2=0.67/0.25=2.7

Demand for pears is cross price elastic with apples (i.e. XED>1)

Just like PED, the absolute value of XED can be:
- *0-1: Inelastic* – Consumers of Good A are relatively unresponsive to a change in the price of Good B (the % change in Q_A will be smaller than the % change in P_B)
- *1: Unit Elastic* – Consumers of Good A will respond proportionally to a change in the price of Good B (the % change in Q_A will be the same as the % change in P_B)
- *>1: Elastic* – Consumers of Good A will be relatively responsive to a change in the price of Good B (the % change in Q_A will be greater than the % change in P_B)

Complementary goods: The XED for complementary goods will always be *NEGATIVE,* because when the price of one complement goes up, the demand for the other will FALL.
- Example: Price of hot dogs rises; the demand for hot dog buns will decrease. XED coefficient will be negative

Substitute goods: The XED for substitutes will always be *POSITIVE,* because when the price of one substitute goes up, the demand for the other will RISE.
- Example: The price of beef rises, the demand for pork will rise. XED coefficient will be positive, reflecting the direct relationship

Income Elasticity of Demand (YED)
Another type of elasticity measures the responsiveness of consumers of a good to a change in the level of their income.

For Example: Imagine a country is going into recession, so incomes of the average household are falling. Demand for new cars is falling, but demand for bicycles is rising. YED is a measure of how responsive consumers' demand for bicycles and cars is to changes in their incomes.

YED=(Percentage change in the quantity of a good)/(Percentage change in consumer's income)
or...
(%ΔQ)/(%ΔY)

Assume the following:
- Incomes in America have fallen by 4%
- Bike sales have risen by 8%
- Car sales have fallen by 3%
- Calculate the YED for bicycles and cars

YED for bikes = 8/-4=-2

Demand for bikes is income elastic

$$YED \text{ for cars} = -3/-4 = 0.75$$

Demand for cars is income inelastic

As with PED and XED, the absolute value of YED can be:

- *0-1: Inelastic* – Demand for the good is relatively unresponsive to changes in consumer income (quantity will change by a smaller percentage than the change in income)
- *1: Unit Elastic* – Demand for the good is proportionally responsive to income changes (quantity will change by the same percentage as the change in income)
- *>1: Elastic* – Demand for the good is relatively responsive to changes in income (quantity will change by a larger percentage than consumers' income)

Normal goods: A normal good is one with a POSITIVE YED coefficient. There is a direct relationship between income and demand.

- Example: As incomes fell, car sales fell as well. If incomes were to rise, car sales would begin to rise. Cars are a normal good.

Inferior goods: An inferior good is one with a NEGATIVE YED coefficient. This is a good that people will buy more of as income falls, and less of as income rises.

- Example: Bicycle transportation is an inferior good, because Americans demanded MORE bicycles as their incomes fell. If income were to rise, bicycle sales would begin to fall.

Price Elasticity of Supply (PES)

This is a measure of the responsiveness of producers to price changes. Since there is always a direct relationship between price and quantity supplied, the PES coefficient will always be positive. PES can be calculated using the same formula as the other types of elasticity:

$$PES = (\text{Percentage change in the quantity supplied})/(\text{Percentage change in the price}) \text{ or...}$$

$$(\%\Delta Qs)/(\%\Delta P)$$

PES will always be positive, since there is a direct relationship between the price of a good and the quantity firms wish to supply.

Consider the following:

- The price of tablet computers rises from $400 to $500
- In the week that follows, the quantity rises from 1 million to 1.1 million
- In the three months that follow, the quantity rise from 1 million to 2 million

PES in the short-run (1 week after price change)
$$= (1.1-1)/1 \div (500-400)/400$$
$$= 0.1/0.25 = 0.4$$

PES in the long run (3 months after price change)
$$= (2-1)/1 \div (500-400)/400$$
$$= 1/0.25 = 4$$

The Determinants of PES
The primary determinant of PES is the amount of time producers have to respond to a price change.
- In the tablet computer market producers were relatively unresponsive to the rise in price in the one week following the price increase (PES equaled only 0.4)
- After three months, producers had the time to increase their production to meet the higher demand, thus they were much more responsive (PES equaled 4)

Three time periods in determining PES
- The Market Period: Immediately after a change in price. Supply is highly inelastic, because firms cannot immediately produce more of a good.
- The short-run: Firms can use their fixed capital more or less intensively, so supply is more slightly more elastic.
- The long run: Firms have time to vary the amount of capital they use, so supply is highly elastic. In the long run an increase in price will result in a much greater increase in Qs than in the market period or the short-run.

Other determinants of PES
In addition to the amount of time following a price change, the following help determine PES:
- *The mobility of resources:* If resources (labor and capital) can be quickly put into or taken out of the production, supply tends to be more elastic. Generally, this applies to low-skilled manufactured goods, the supply of which is more elastic than high-tech, capital-intensive manufactured goods.
- *The ability to store stocks:* If large inventories can be kept, producers can respond to price rises by drawing on those inventories to meet rising demand and to price declines by adding to inventories in response to falling demand. Goods that can be stored tend to have more elastic supply than perishable, non-storable goods.

Applications of PES
Similar to PED, knowledge of PES can help businesses and the government better plan for the anticipated price changes to particular goods.
- *Business firms:* If a producer expects the price of his product to change in the future, he will want to adjust his output accordingly. Being able to adjust output in a timely manner to price changes is key to maximizing a firm's profits.
- *Government:* A government must consider the PES for a good if it is considering intervening in the market for that good in any way. For example, if a government is considering imposing price controls (maximum or minimum prices) on an agricultural commodity, the PES should be considered so any changes in output resulting from the government controlled price could be anticipated.

Chapter 4 – Government Intervention in Markets

Government Intervention
- Indirect taxes
- Subsidies
- Price Controls

The Role of Government in the Market Economy
Up to this point, we have examined how *free* markets work.

A free market is one without any government control or intervention. The price and output is determined by the interactions of buyers and sellers

However, not all markets are completely free. Governments tend to intervene often to influence several variables in markets for particular goods, such as:
- Taxing the good to discourage consumption or raise revenues: *Indirect taxes*
- Paying producers of the good to reduce costs or encourage the good's production: *Subsidies*
- Reducing the price of the good below its free market equilibrium to benefit consumers: *Price Ceilings*
- Raising the price of a good above its free market equilibrium to benefit producers: *Price Floors*

When governments intervene in the free market, the level of output and price that results may NOT be the allocatively efficient level. In other words, government intervention may lead to a misallocation of society's resources.

Indirect Taxes
An indirect tax is one placed by the government on the producers of a particular good.
- Consumers will pay the tax *indirectly* through producers
- An indirect tax will be shared by both consumers and producers

The effect of an indirect tax on the market for a good: Examine the market for pencils.
- Assume the government decides to place a $0.50 tax on pencil production to raise revenue to support the pen industry.
- The tax is an additional cost for pencil producers, so the supply of pencils decreases.
- MC and Supply will shift UP by $0.50
- The price of pencils increases from $1.25 to $1.55.
- Once the tax is paid, pencil producers get to keep just $1.05

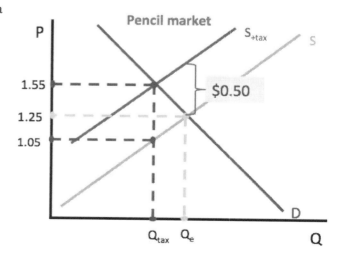

Determining the Effect of Indirect Taxes
As we saw above, a tax reduces the supply of a good and increases the price. The following points should also be observed.

- The price of the good does not increase by the full amount of the tax
- The producers of the good do not keep the full price paid by consumers, as they must pay the tax
- There is a loss of total welfare in the market resulting from the tax.

The $0.50 tax on pencils…

- Increase the price consumers pay by $0.30.
- Decreases the price producers get to keep by $0.20.
- Decreases the output from Qe to Qtax
- Imposes a burden on consumers equal to the area above 1.25 and below 1.55.
- Imposes a burden on producers equal to the area below 1.25 and above 1.05.
- Raises government revenue equal to the consumer and producer burden combined.
- Causes a net loss of total welfare equal to the triangle to the right of the tax revenue.

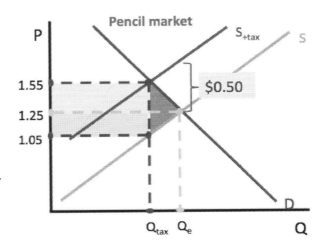

The Effects of an Indirect Tax and PED
Consumers paid $0.30 of the $0.50 tax and producers paid only $0.20. The tax was shared, but consumers paid the larger share. Determining who will pay the larger share of a tax requires us to examine the price elasticity of demand for the good being taxed.

- *If demand is relatively elastic:* Producers will bear the larger burden of the tax. Firms will not be able to raise the price by much out of fear of losing all their customers, therefore price will not increase by much, but producers will get to keep less of what consumers pay.
- *If demand is relatively inelastic:* Consumes will bear the larger burden of the tax. Firms will be able to pass most of the tax onto consumers, who are not very responsive to the higher price, thus will continue to consume close to what they were before the tax.
- *Elasticity and government revenue:* The implication for government of the above analysis is that if a tax is meant to raise revenue, it is better placed on an inelastic good rather than an elastic good. Taxing elastic goods will reduce the quantity sold and thus not raise much revenue.

Examine the effects of the same $1 tax on the two goods below, one a highly elastic good, the other a highly inelastic good.

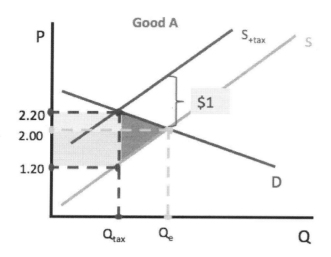
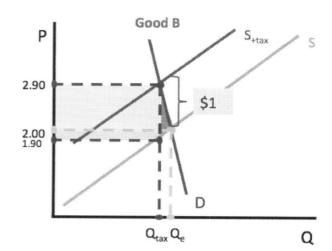

The Effects of an Indirect Tax and PED

Observations:
The $1 tax on Good A (highly elastic demand):
- $0.80 is paid by produces, and only $0.20 by consumers
- Quantity falls dramatically.
- The loss of welfare (gray triangle) is large
- Revenue raised is small due to the large decrease in Q

The $1 tax on Good B (highly inelastic demand):
- $0.90 is paid by consumers, and only $0.10 by producers
- Quantity does not fall by much
- The loss of welfare (gray triangle) is small
- Revenue raised is greater than Good A because the quantity does not fall by much

Taxing goods with relatively inelastic demand will raise more revenue and lead to a smaller loss of total welfare, while taxing goods with elastic demand will lead to a larger decrease in quantity and a greater loss of total welfare.

The Effects of an Indirect Tax in Linear Supply Equations
A tax is an additional cost placed on producers in a market. Therefore, a tax will affect the supply curve AND the supply equation. One way to think about a tax is that it is a payment made by the producers to the government of a particular amount AFTER consumers have bought the good. Therefore, to show the effect of a tax on a supply equation, we must subtract the amount of the tax from the price consumers paid.

Consider the supply of bread in a small town: *Qs=-200+150P*
Assume a $1 tax is imposed on bread producers. This means that whatever consumers pay (*P*), producers will keep $1 less. The new supply equation is therefore:

$$Qs=-200+150(P-1)$$

This can be simplified:

$$Qs=-200+150P-150$$

The new supply of bread is:

$$Qs=-350+150P$$

A $1 tax on the production of bread cause the supply to decrease.
The new supply of bread is:

$$Qs=-350+150P$$

Notice:

- The 'c' variable in the equation decreased. This it the Q-intercept of supply, which is now lower on the Q axis, meaning supply has shifted to the left by 150 units, or up by $1.
- The 'd' variable has not changed. The tax does not change the *responsiveness* of producers to price changes. They will still supply 150 more loaves for every $1 increase in price.

Calculating the effect of a tax on equilibrium: Assume demand for bread is: $Qd=600-50P$ *The tax has no effect on demand, only supply.*			
Before the tax:	600-50P=-200+150P 800=200P **P=$4** Qd=600-50(4) **Qd=400**	**After the tax:**	600-50P=-350+150P 950=200P **P=$4.75** Qd=600-50(4.75) **Qd=237.5**

Per-unit Subsidies

A subsidy, in contrast to a tax, is a payment *from the government to producers* for each unit produced

The effect of a per-unit subsidy on the market for a good: Assume the government places a $0.50 subsidy on the production of pens.

- Supply shifts 'down' by $0.50, since the subsidy reduces the marginal costs of pen producers.
- The price consumers pay falls from $2 to $1.70.
- The price producers receive for each pen is the $1.70 consumers pay plus the $0.50 subsidy, or $2.20
- There is a greater quantity of pens produced

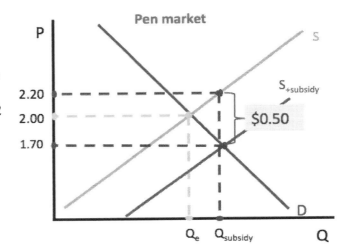

Determining the Effect of Per-unit Subsidies
As we saw above, a subsidy increases the supply of a good and reduces the price. The following points should also be observed.

- The price of the good does not decrease by the full amount of the subsidy
- Pen consumers enjoy some of the benefit of the good, but producers also benefit
- There is a loss of total welfare in the market resulting from the cost of the subsidy exceeding the benefit

The $0.50 subsidy for pens…
- Decreases the price consumers pay to $1.70
- Increases the price producers receive to $2.20
- Increases the output from Qe to Qsubsidy
- Increases Consumer Surplus by the area below 2.00, above 1.70 and out to Qsubsidy
- Increases Producer Surplus by the area above 2.00, below 2.20 and out to Qsubsidy
- Costs tax payers an amount represented by the rectangle below 2.20, above 1.70 and out to Qsubsidy

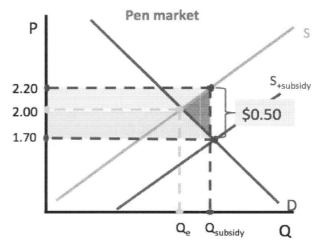

Causes a net loss of total welfare equal to the gray area (since the total cost to taxpayers exceeded the total increase in consumer and producer surplus)

The Effects of a Per-unit Subsidy in Linear Supply Equations
A subsidy is a payment to producers *for each unit produced,* therefore it reduces the costs of producing each unit of goods. Lower costs increase supply and affect the supply equation
- One way to think about a subsidy is that it is a payment to producers above and beyond the price consumers pay.
- Therefore, to show the effect of a subsidy on a supply equation, we must ADD the amount of the subsidy to the price consumers paid.

Consider the supply of bread in a small town: $Qs=-200+150P$
Assume a $1 subsidy is provided to bread producers. This means that whatever consumers pay (*P*), producers will receive $1 more. The new supply equation is therefore:

$$Qs=-200+150(P+1)$$

This can be simplified:

$$Qs=-200+150P+150$$

The new supply of bread is:

$$Qs=-50+150P$$

A $1 subsidy to the producers of bread causes the supply to increase.
The new supply of bread is:

$$Qs=-50+150P$$

Notice:
- The 'c' variable in the equation increased. This it the Q-intercept of supply, which is now closer to the origin on the Q axis, meaning supply has shifted to the right by 150 units
- The 'd' variable has not changed. The subsidy does not change the *responsiveness* of producers to price changes. They will still supply 150 more loaves for every $1 price increase

Calculating the effect of a tax on equilibrium: Assume demand for bread is: Qd=600-50P			
The tax has no effect on demand, only supply.			
Before the subsidy:	600-50P=-200+150P 800=200P **P=$4** Qd=600-50(4) **Qd=400**	After the subsidy:	600-50P=-50+150P 650=200P **P=$3.25** Qd=600-50(3.25) **Qd=437.5**

The Effects of Taxes and Subsidies on Consumers and Producers
We can determine how much of the tax burden was born by consumers and producers:

Effect of the tax
- The price increased from $4.00 to $4.75; meaning consumers paid $0.75 of the $1.00 tax.
- Producers got to keep just $3.75, meaning they paid just $0.25 of the $1.00 tax

Effect of the subsidy:
- Price went down from $4.00 to $3.25; meaning consumers received $0.75 of the $1.00 subsidy.
- Producers received $4.25, meaning they enjoyed $0.25 of the $1.00 subsidy.

Before the tax and the subsidy:	600-50P=-200+150P 800=200P **P=$4** Qd=600-50(4) **Qd=400**	After the tax:	600-50P=-350+150P 950=200P **P=$4.75** Qd=600-50(4.75) **Qd=237.5**
		After the subsidy:	600-50P=-50+150P 650=200P **P=$3.25** Qd=600-50(3.25) **Qd=437.5**

Price Controls
Another form government intervention might take in a market is price controls.

Price Ceiling (left graph): This is a maximum price, set below the equilibrium price, meant to help consumers of a product by keeping the price low.

Price Floor (right graph): This is a minimum price, set above the equilibrium price, meant to help producers of a product by keeping the price high.

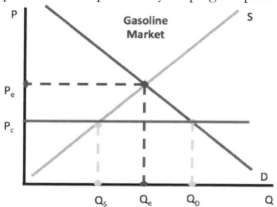 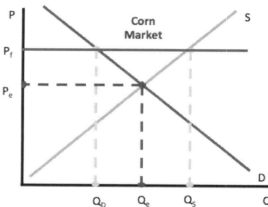

The Effects of a Price Ceiling
When a government lowers the price of a good to help consumers, there are several effects that we can observe in the market. Assume the government has intervened in the market for gasoline to make transportation more affordable for the nation's households

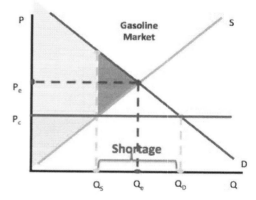

On consumers:
- Quantity demanded increases (Qd)
- The lower price leads to an increase in consumer surplus, which is now the area above Pc and below the demand curve, left of Qs
- The lower quantity means some consumers who want to will not be able to buy the good

On Producers:
- The lower price means less producer surplus (the triangle below Pc, above supply curve)
- The lower quantity means some producers will have to leave the market and output will decline (Qs)

On the market:
- Overall, not enough gasoline is produced, and is the market is allocatively inefficient. The gray triangle represents the loss of total welfare resulting from the price ceiling.

The Effects of a Price Floor
When a government raises the price of a good to help producers, there are several effects that we can observe in the market. Assume the government has intervened in the market for corn to help farmers sell their crop at a price that allows them to earn a small profit.

On consumers:
- Quantity demanded decreases (Qd)
- The higher price means there is less consumer surplus

On Producers:
- Quantity supplied increases (Qs)
- The higher price means there is more producer surplus, but since consumers only demand Qd, there is an excess supply of unsold corn (Qd-Qs)

On the market:
- Overall, the market produces too much corn and is thus allocatively inefficient. The increase in producer surplus is smaller than the decrease in consumer surplus. The total loss of welfare is represented by the gray triangle.

Calculating the Effects of Price Controls using Linear Equations
As with taxes and subsidies, we can use linear supply and demand equations to calculate the effects of price ceilings and price floors. Once again, assume demand and supply for bread is:

$$Qd=600-50P \text{ and } Qs=-200+150P$$

As we have already shown, the current equilibrium price is $4 and the quantity is 400 loaves. Assume the government wishes to help households afford bread, so imposes a price ceiling of $3 on bread. To determine the impact on the market, we must simply put $3 into both equations.

$$Qd=600-50(3)=450 \text{ loaves}$$
$$Qs=-200+150(3)=250 \text{ loaves}$$

The $3.00 price ceiling will create a shortage of 200 loaves of bread.
- Producers will reduce their output of bread and more consumers will wish to buy bread.
- The price ceiling took a market that was *efficient* and made it *inefficient. Not enough resources are allocated towards bread production as a result of the price ceiling.*

Next, assume that the government determines that $4 is too cheap for bread, and producers need the price to be higher. The government imposes a price floor of $5 in the market. To determine the impact on the market, we must simply put $5 into both equations.

$$Qd=600-50(5)=350 \text{ loaves}$$
$$Qs=-200+150(5)=550 \text{ loaves}$$

The $5.00 price floor will create a surplus of 200 loaves of bread.

- Producers will increase their production of bread to take advantage of the now higher prices it is commanding in the market.
- Consumers will reduce the quantity of bread they demand due to the now higher price.
- The price floor took an efficient market and made it allocatively inefficient. *Too many resources are now being allocated towards bread production!*

Conclusion*: Price controls rarely increase efficiency or total welfare in a market. They result in either shortages (price ceilings) or surpluses (price floors), and therefore lead to a net loss in total welfare for society. Some benefit, but many suffer.*

Buffer Stock Schemes

A buffer stock scheme is a form of government intervention, often used in the markets for certain agricultural commodities, which combines price controls and subsidies.

A buffer stock scheme: A policy that regulates the price of non-perishable agricultural commodities to keep it within a narrow range that is deemed desirable for both producers and consumers. *Consider the market for coffee below:*

There is a price ceiling above the current equilibrium, and a price floor below the current equilibrium. At present, neither is binding.

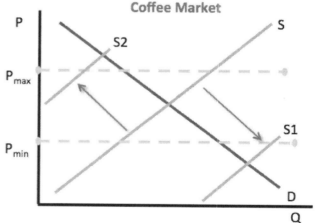

- In a good year: The supply of coffee increases to S1. The price floor now becomes binding. The government can *buy up the surplus* that is created and put it in storage. This keeps the price above Pmin.
- In a bad year: The supply of coffee falls to S2. The price ceiling now becomes binding. The government can *release its buffer stock from the good years* on the market to increase supply and keep the price below Pmax
- Obstacles: High storage costs, only works for non-perishable goods, may reduce innovation in agricultural markets

Chapter 5 – Market Failure

Market Failure
- Market failure as a failure to allocate resources efficiently
- The meaning of externalities
- Negative externalities of production and consumption
- Positive externalities of production and consumption
- Lack of public goods
- Common access resources and the thread to sustainability
- Asymmetric information
- Abuse of monopoly power

Introduction to Market Failure
Up to this point in the course we have focused on the *efficiency* of the free market.
- Markets are efficient because, when in equilibrium, they are *allocatively efficient*
- The socially optimal amount of output will be produced: Marginal Social Benefit will equal Marginal Social Cost
- When governments intervene in free markets (indirect taxes, subsidies, price controls), resources become misallocated and there is a loss of total welfare.

Market Failure Definition: Markets are NOT always efficient. There are several circumstances under which resources will be *mis-allocated* by the free market. In other words, either *too much* of a good will be produced or *not enough* will be produced by the free market. Examples of market failures include:
- Negative Externalities of Production and Consumption
- Positive Externalities of Production and Consumption
- Lack of Public Goods
- Common Access Resources and the Tragedy of the Commons
- Asymmetric Information
- Abuse of Monopoly Power

Externalities
One way markets fail to achieve allocative efficiency arises from the existence of *externalities* in the market for a god

Externality Definition: An externality exists any time the production or consumption of a good creates spillover benefits or costs on a third party not involved in the market. In such cases, resources will either be under-allocated (positive externalities) or over-allocated (negative externalities) towards the production of certain goods.

Examples of Positive Externalities (known as merit goods)	Examples of Negative Externalities (known as demerit goods)
Receiving a college education makes the consumer more likely to contribute to the well-being of society as a whole	Driving sports-utility vehicles contributes to traffic and contributes more to global warming
Riding bicycles to work reduces congestion on the roads and makes for less traffic for everyone else	Producing electricity using coal creates greenhouse gas emissions and air pollution
Getting vaccines against communicable diseases reduces the chance you will get others sick	Smoking cigarettes contributes to lung disease among not just the smokers, but those who suffer from second-hand smoke

Negative Externalities of Production
In each of the examples from the table there is a good or service being produced or consumed by one group of people that creates either costs or benefits for another group of people. We will examine four types of externalities now, beginning with…

Negative Externalities of Production: These arise when the production of a good creates spillover costs on a third party, which is often times the environment as a whole. The Marginal Social Cost of producing a good is greater than the Marginal Private Cost of producing it… Example: A polluting industry.

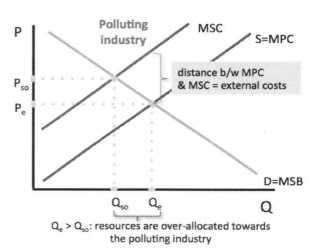

$Q_e > Q_{so}$: resources are over-allocated towards the polluting industry

In the graph…
- MPC = The private costs of producing the good
- MSC = the cost to society of producing the good, includes the MPC plus any external costs
- Q_e = the actual output in the market
- Q_{so} = The socially optimal output in the market
- P_e = the equilibrium price in the market
- P_{so} = the socially optimal price if all social costs were considered in the good's production

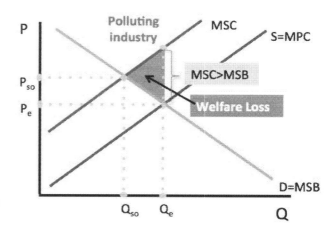

A polluting industry creates costs for society that are not paid by the polluting firm. These *external costs of production* may include:
- Greenhouse gas emissions which contribute to global warming

- Air pollution
- Contributions to lung disease and cancer rates among the population
- Water pollution which destroys fish stocks
- Soil contamination that harms agricultural productivity.

The existence of all these externalities creates a social cost that exceeds the private cost!
- As a result, there is a loss of total welfare in the industry represented by the gray triangle.
- At the equilibrium output of Qe, the marginal social cost exceeds the marginal social benefit, meaning…

Too much of the good is being produced by the free market! This is a market failure!

Negative Externalities of Consumption

Some goods are over-*consumed* by the free market. This would be the case if the process of consuming a good creates spillover costs on a third party. The classic example of a *negative consumption externality* is cigarettes.

Consider the market seen here:
- The Marginal Private Benefit (MPB) of smoking cigarettes is greater than the Marginal Social Benefit (MSB)
- Smoking creates costs (negative benefits) on non-smokers, so society benefits as a whole less than the smokers themselves
- There are no externalities in the production of cigarettes, so the supply curve represents the private costs and the social costs.
- The equilibrium price (Pe) is greater than the price would if demand represented the social benefits of smoking (Pso)
- The equilibrium quantity (Qe) is greater than the socially optimal quantity (Qso)

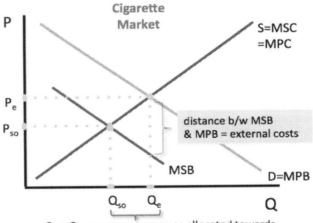

$Q_e > Q_{so}$: resources are over-allocated towards the cigarette industry

Smoking harms third parties who do not buy or sell cigarettes, therefore this is a negative consumption externality.

Notice on the graph:
- At Qe (the actual quantity of cigarettes consumed in a free market), the MSC of smoking exceeds the MSB.
- Too many cigarettes are being produced and consumed at Qe,

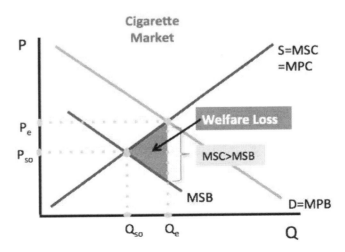

resulting in a loss of total welfare equal to the gray triangle.

Resources will be over-allocated towards the production and consumption of cigarettes by the free market. This is a market failure!

Government Responses to Negative Externalities

Whenever a market fails by allocating *too many* resources towards the production of the good, the government can potentially *improve market efficiency* by intervening to reduce the quantity produced and consumed to a more socially optimal level (where MSB=MSC). Methods a government might take to correct a negative externality include:

- *Corrective taxes:* This is a per-unit tax on a good meant to reduce the supply, increase the price, and reduce the quantity demanded to a more socially optimal level. Unlike a tax on a good that is produced *efficiently* by the free market, this is a *corrective tax* because it is meant to correct a failing market and help the market achieve a higher level of efficiency.
- *Regulation/Legislation:* Laws that limit the quantity of a good produced or require it to be produced in an environmentally friendly way may increase the costs of production to firms and reduce the quantity to a more socially optimal level.
- *Banning:* Many goods that create negative externalities are simply banned. Examples include: Drinking among minors, narcotics, prostitution, automatic weapons, etc....
- *Tradable Permits:* Issuing permits to producers of goods that create negative environmental externalities will create a physical limit on the amount of pollution or of the harmful activity, reducing the overall cost to society of the activity.

Government Responses to Negative Externalities – Corrective Taxes

A tax meant to correct a market failure is sometimes referred to as a *Pigouvian Tax,* after the economist *Arthur Pigou,* who first proposed using taxes to reduce the output of harmful goods.

- Recall that a tax is a determinant of supply,
- A tax on a good that created externalities of production or consumption will *increase the marginal private costs of production and reduce the supply to a level closer to the marginal social costs (which include all external costs).*

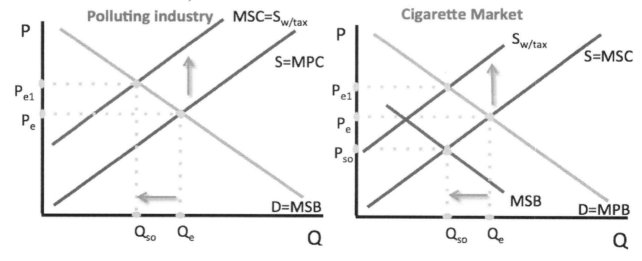

The tax reduces the supply of both goods, causing the equilibrium price to rise and the quantity demanded to fall. If the size of the tax reflects the size of the external costs, then the new equilibrium output (Qe) will equal the socially optimal level of output (Qso)

Evaluation of Corrective Taxes
Corrective taxes are a popular response to negative externalities among economist, but among policy-makers, they are rarely popular. Some arguments against corrective taxes include:

- *Higher costs for producers:* Producers face higher costs, and therefore will reduce their output of the goods being taxed. This is bad for business.
- *Higher prices for consumers:* Consumers of the goods being taxed face higher prices, reducing consumer surplus and the real incomes of households. For some goods (such as electricity) this could place a major financial burden on households.
- *Less employment:* As the taxed industries reduce their output, they may be forced to lay off workers, increasing unemployment in the economy.
- *Loss of competitiveness in global market:* This is a major one. Policy-makers fear that if *they* impose taxes on their nation's producers, but other nations' governments do not impose taxes on their producers, then the domestic industries will suffer while foreign producers thrive. International cooperation on the implementation of corrective taxes could eliminate this problem, but there have been very few examples of such cooperation.

Government Responses to Negative Externalities – Tradable Permits
A second method for reducing the negative externalities arising from production or consumption of certain goods is the use of tradable permits.

- For example, in Europe there is a market for permits to emit carbon dioxide, a greenhouse gas widely believed to contribute to global warming. *Here's how it works…*

1. A government or multi-national governing body issues or auctions off permits to polluting industries that allow them to emit a certain amount of carbon.
2. Some firms pollute beyond their permitted amount, so will either have to acquire more permits or reduce their emissions
3. To acquire more permits, they must buy them from in the market from firms that do not need all of their permits
4. The supply of permits is fixed and determined by the government, the demand for permits therefore determines the price of pollution. The more firms want to pollute, the more expensive it becomes to pollute.
5. There is a strong incentive for firms to reduce their emissions, because they can then sell the permits they do not need, adding to firm profit.

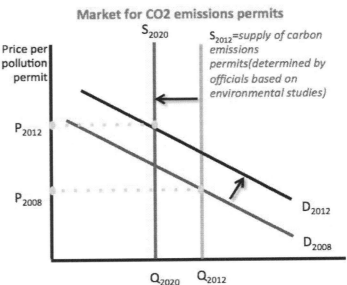

A tradable permit scheme has several advantages over corrective taxes, and some disadvantages…

Advantages of tradable permits:
- Creates a strong incentive to *reduce* pollution, since permits can be sold off for profit
- Creates a clear *price* for pollution, internalizing the costs that firms would have externalized without the scheme.
- Places a clear limit on the *quantity* of pollution that will be created each year
- Price of permits can be increased over time by reducing the number of permits available.

Disadvantages of tradable permits:
- The price of permits is determined by the free market, and may be too low to create strong incentives to reduce pollution
- The amount of permits is decided by government, and may be too high if polluting industries are allowed to influence policy
- It is costly and difficult to monitor industries to make sure everyone who pollutes has the permits to do so.

Government Responses to Negative Externalities – Regulation

Regulation of polluting or harmful industries is another option for governments to attempt and promote a more socially optimal level of output of a demerit good. Some factors to consider when a government regulates an industry include:
- *Monitoring:* The government must monitor emissions of polluters, which can be costly and difficult.
- *Enforcement:* The government must have a way to enforce legislation on polluters.
- *Penalties:* The penalties for violations must be significant enough to dissuade firms from ignoring legislation
- *Incentives:* If the penalty is not harsh enough, the firm will simply ignore regulations and pollute anyway. The fine must be greater than the cost of pollution abatement, otherwise firms will keep polluting.

Effect of regulation: Similar to a tax or the requirement that firms must buy permits for pollution, regulation will add to the cost of producing harmful goods. Firms face higher costs in adhering to regulations, reducing the supply of demerit goods and creating incentives for firms to produce goods in more environmentally and socially responsible ways.

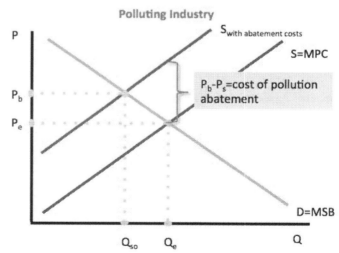

The intended effect of government regulations of externalizing industries is to force the polluters to incur costs associated with pollution control. Firms forced to reduce their pollution will face higher costs, shifting the market supply curve for a polluting product to the left. Equilibrium quantity should fall closer to the socially optimal level.

Positive Externalities of Production

A positive externality of production exists if the production of a good or service provides spillover benefits to a third part not involved in the market. For example, consider the market for ***ECO-TOURISM.***

- In many parts of the world, including in the Amazon rainforest, in Costa Rica, in Malaysian Borneo, Western Canada and elsewhere, a large eco-tourism industry has developed.
- This industry provides paying customers with the experience of outdoor adventures in nature
- But the existence of this industry creates positive benefits for society beyond those who pay for the experience.
- Positive externalities of eco-tourism include:
  - ➢ Forests left standing act as a "carbon sink", absorbing CO_2 emitted from the production of other consumer goods.
  - ➢ Protection of eco-systems that might otherwise be exploited or developed
  - ➢ Wildlife populations may remain protected and intact whereas they otherwise may dwindle due to habitat destruction and over-hunting
  - ➢ Water resources (rivers, lakes) are protected, allowing downstream users to benefit from clean water for cooking, cleaning, drinking, etc....

The existence of a positive production externality can be illustrated graphically as a market in which the Marginal Private Cost of production (MPC) is greater than the Marginal Social Cost of production (MSC). As a result, the free market will provide a quantity of the good that is less than the socially optimal quantity.

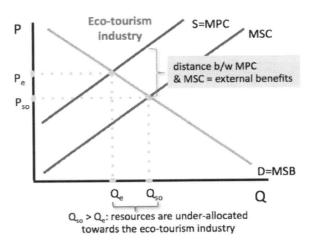

In the market on the right:
- Operating a business in the industry is expensive, so the MPC is relatively high.
- There are external benefits of operating an eco-tourism business, which are reflected in the lower MSC.
- The equilibrium price (Pe) is higher than what is socially optimal (Pso). The quantity demanded would be greater for eco-tourism if the price were lower.
- The equilibrium quantity (Qe) is less than what is socially optimal (Qso). Society would be better off with more businesses offering eco-tourism services.

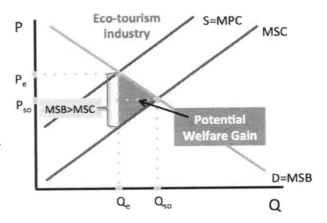

Because the free market will provide not enough eco-tourism services, there is an area of *potential welfare gain* in the market diagram. If a greater quantity of the *merit good* were produced and consumed, society as a whole would be better off.

At the equilibrium quantity and price:
- The MSB is greater than the MSC. Society benefits more than it costs to provide Qe, resources are under-allocated towards eco-tourism
- Society stands to gain an amount of welfare equal to the gray triangle if more eco-tourism can be provided.
- The price (Pe) is too high, and therefor the equilibrium quantity demanded (Qe) too low.

Increased provision of merit goods like eco-tourism would benefit society as a whole

Positive Externalities of Consumption
A positive externality of consumption exists if the consumption of a good or service provides spillover benefits to a third part not involved in the market. For example, consider the market for *EDUCATION*.
- Getting an education provides many benefits for the student, such as better job opportunities, higher pay, an earlier retirement and better travel opportunities
- However, receiving an education also benefits society as a whole.
- Positive externalities of education include:
  - ➤ An educated citizen will be more productive in his or her life, contributing more to national output,
  - ➤ He or she will pay more in taxes, which go towards providing benefits for everyone in society, even those without an education.
  - ➤ He or she is more likely to become a business owner, offering employment opportunities to others in society that may not otherwise have been provided.

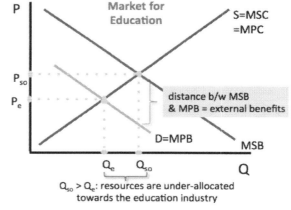

Education is a merit good, which provides spillover benefits to society as a whole.

Because there are external benefits of consuming education:
- The Marginal Social Benefits of receiving an education (MSB) are greater than the Marginal Private Benefits of receiving an education (MPB).
- If left to the free market, too few people will receive the highest levels of education

In the market for education:
- Private demand for education is equal to the marginal private benefit.
- The quantity of education society will consume if it is left entirely to the free market is Qe, but this is less than what is socially optimal (Qso)

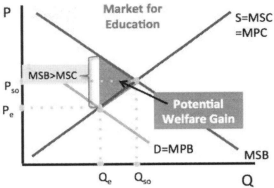

- There are external benefits of receiving an education, represented by the vertical distance between MPB and MSB

Anytime the free market provides too little of a good or service, there is a potential gain in total welfare of the good being produced at a greater quantity.

At the equilibrium price and quantity:
- The marginal social benefit of education is greater than the marginal social cost, indicating that not enough education is being provided.
- At the socially optimal quantity (Qso), the MSB=MSC, indicating that this is the allocatively efficient level of education to provide.
- If demand were greater, the price would be higher and more institutions would provide education, increasing the quantity supplied.

Increased provision of merit goods like education would benefit society as a whole

Government Responses to Positive Externalities
When a market fails by *under-allocating resources* towards the production of a good, society stands to benefit from increasing the production and consumption of the good in the market. Therefore, government policies aimed at increasing either the supply or the demand for the good can improve efficiency in the market for merit goods. Such policies include:
- *Corrective subsidies (to producers):* A subsidy is a payment from the government to producers. Subsidies lower the marginal private costs of production, increasing the supply, reducing the price and increasing the quantity demanded for the good being subsidized.
- *Corrective subsidies (to consumers):* A subsidy to consumers of a good will increase the marginal private benefit of consumption (since individuals now get paid to buy a good) and increase the demand for the good. The higher price incentivizes firms to provide a greater quantity, resulting in a more efficient allocation of resources towards the good
- *Government provision:* Many merit goods are provided by the government, such as education, health care, infrastructure like bridges and airports, police security, and so on.
- *Positive advertising:* Government programs that educate consumers about the positive private and social benefits of a good may increase demand for the good, incentivizing firms to produce more of it. Examples include healthy eating campaigns, safe sex campaigns (to encourage condom use) promoting flue shots (and other vaccines), and so on…

Corrective Subsidies

A subsidy to producers reduces the marginal private costs of production and increases the supply of the good being subsidized. In the markets below, the government is subsidizing eco-tourism providers and private schools. Both subsidies lead to a greater equilibrium quantity, a lower equilibrium price, and an increase in total welfare in society.

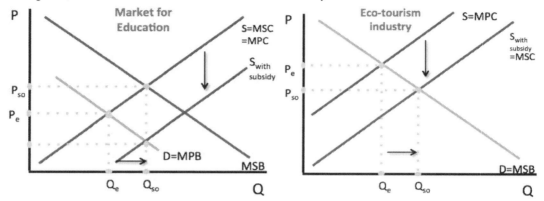

Public Goods

So far we have heard about markets failing when they:

- *Produce too much of a good (negative externalities)*
- *Produce too little of a good (positive externalities)*

But what if a market produced NONE of a good. A good that is not provided by the free market AT ALL is known as a PUBLIC GOOD.

Public Good: A good that provides benefits to society which are non-rivalrous, and the benefits of which are non-excludable by the provider of the good. Because of these characteristics, public goods will not be provide by the free market at all (hence, represent a market failure)

To be considered public, a good must be:

- *Non-rivalrous in consumption:* This means that one consumer's enjoyment of the benefits of a good does not diminish any other consumer's enjoyment of its benefits.
- *Non-excludable by the provider:* This means that once a good has been provided, it is not possible to exclude any individuals from enjoying its benefits. In other words, you can't make individuals pay for the good once it is made available. *There will be free-riders,* or individuals who enjoy the good's benefits without ever paying for it!

Examples of Public Goods

To find examples of public goods, all we have to do is walk out our front door and look around. Many of the goods and services a government provides its citizens using tax money are examples of public goods. These may include:

- *Infrastructure:* Roads, sidewalks, street lights, power lines, sewage systems, train tracks... many of these goods are non-excludable and non-rivalrous, therefore are unlikely to be provided by the free market. Government must provide such goods so that society can enjoy their benefits.

- *Parks:* Think of the last time you walked through a *public park*. Did you have to pay to get in? (If not, then it was non-excludable). Did your enjoyment of the park prevent others from enjoying it? (If not, then it was non-rivalrous). Public parks are an example of public goods.
- *Fire and Police Protection:* If your house catches on fire, do you have to call a private fire-fighting firm to come put it out? The reason you don't is because the *benefits of having fire protection are non-rivalrous*. Putting the fire in your house out will benefit your neighbors, whose houses are less likely to burn down. Police protection is the same way. Without government-provided police force, society as a whole would be unsafe because very few people would choose to hire private security. The benefits of police protection are *non-rivalrous and non-excludable.*
- *National Defense:* An army, navy and air force provide citizens with protection, which, once provided, individuals within the nation cannot be excluded from benefiting from. One person's safety does not diminish others', so defense is non-excludable and non-rivalrous: a purely public good.

Common Access Resources

In addition to *merit goods, demerit goods and public goods*, a third type of market failure arises from the existence of common access resources:

Common Access Resources: Those "gifts of nature" over which there is no private ownership, and therefore no effective means of regulating the use of the resource.
Examples of common access resources include:

- *Fish in the sea*
- *Trees in a forest*
- *Common pastureland*
- *Fresh water in aquifers or in rivers*

In each of these cases, the lack of ownership over the resources creates an incentive for potential users to exploit them to the fullest extent possible, so as to extract as much benefit as possible before other users extract and exploit the resource. This is known as *The Tragedy of the Commons*

Common Access Resources – possible solutions
When there exist a common resource, for which there is no private owner, the incentive among rational users of that resources is to exploit it to the fullest potential in order to maximize their own self gain before the resource is depleted.

- The tragedy of the commons, therefore, is that common resources will inevitably be depleted due to humans' self-interested behavior, leaving us with shortages in key resources essential to human survival.
- This represents a market failure because, without allocation of property rights over or effective management of common access resources, they will be exploited *unsustainably*

Sustainability: The ability of an activity or a resource to endure for the use and enjoyment of future generations.

Possible Solutions to the Tragedy of the Commons:	
Privatization:	Assigning private ownership over a resource creates an incentive among the private owners to protect and manage its use in a sustainable manner, so as to benefit from its existence into the future.
Government management:	Strict government control over the access to and use of common resources may limit access to them to a sustainable level.
Tradable permits:	Issuing permits to private users to allow a certain amount of extraction in a period of time may limit the exploitation of the resource to sustainable level.

Asymmetric Information as a Market Failure

Yet another type of market failure arises from the existence of *asymmetric information.*

Asymmetric Information: When the one party in an economic transaction (either the buyer or the seller) knows important information about the good or service that he withholds from the other party.

- Without perfect knowledge, buyers may not buy the optimal quantity of a product, thus resources may be misallocated towards its production and consumption.
- Without all the information about a product, Demand (marginal private benefit) may be greater than what is socially optimal (marginal social benefit), resulting external costs for society caused by consumers demanding too much of certain goods.

Market Failures arising from Information Asymmetry	
Adverse Selection:	Typical market failure in the market for insurance; if the buyer of insurance does not share with the insurer complete information about the level of risk he or she presents, insurance will be provided at too low a cost to too many risky individuals. The cost of covering the dishonest are thereby shared by the more honest customers, for whom the cost of insurance is, as a result, higher than it would be otherwise.
Moral Hazard:	Also a type of information asymmetry, if the consequences of one's actions are born by society as a whole or by a third party, rather than by the individual himself, he is more likely to take risky actions that he would not take if the consequences were fully born by himself. For example, if you have a rental car with full insurance, you are more likely to drive recklessly than in your own car, on which you have a high co-pay.

The US Financial Crisis as a Market Failure

What follows is a short interpretation of how the global financial crisis of 2007-2008 was the result of information asymmetry and therefore a market failure

- In the US and other countries, households were offered "sub-prime" loans, which allowed those who would not have traditionally qualified for a home loan to borrow money and buy a house.
- Borrowers were told that the debt they were taking on would not be a problem due to the fact that "home prices always rise", information that was thought to be factual by most who bought homes at the time.
- Banks "bundled" these loans into securities that they sold to investors all over the world, who assumed that the lending banks were correct in their assumption that house prices would continue to rise.
- Developers built houses in record numbers based on the assumption that they'd be able to sell them at higher and higher prices.
- Supply of houses grew faster than demand, and eventually house prices began to fall.
- Borrowers found they could not make their monthly payments because their loans were "adjustable rate" meaning they required higher payments over time, causing foreclosures to increase and the supply of houses for sale to grow even more, forcing prices down even further.
- Now investors and banks all over the world hold securities made up of bad loans to Americans that were made based on the incorrect assumption that house prices would always rise. With bad assets on their "balance sheets" banks are unable to make new loans to consumers and firms, so spending in the economy has slowed, meaning recession and high unemployment

The asymmetric information at the root of the financial crisis was the belief that "home prices always rise". When this turned out to be false, there were too many homes on the market and trillions of dollars in households' investments were lost, throwing the global economy into a recession.

The Abuse of Monopoly Power as a Market Failure

The final type of market failure we will examine is the abuse of monopoly power by firms that control a large share of a particular market.

Monopoly Power: When a single firm controls a large share of the total market for a particular good, that firm is able to charge a HIGHER PRICE and produce a LOWER QUANTITY than what is socially optimal.

The source of monopoly power arises from a large firm's price-making abilities.

- In more competitive markets, hundreds of small firms compete with one another for the business of consumers.
- Competition forces firms to produce their goods efficiently (at a low cost) and sell their goods for a low price
- Without competition, monopolists are not forced to produce at the lowest cost, nor do they have to sell for the lowest price.

Monopolists (or firms with significant market power), are both productively and allocatively inefficient, since without competition, such firms are able to charge higher prices and produce smaller quantities!

The Abuse of Monopoly Power as a Market Failure – Graphical Portrayal
A monopolist's price-making power allows it to produce a lower quantity and charge a higher price than what is achieved in a more competitive market.

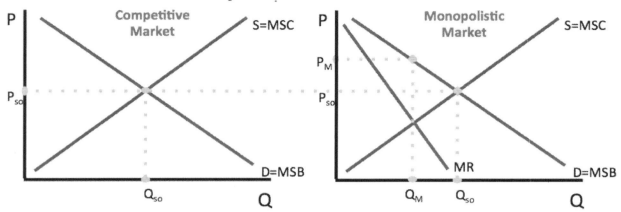

Observe in the graphs above:
- In the competitive market, the price and quantity are always determined by the intersection of demand and supply, which represent MSC and MSB, and therefore is allocatively efficient.
- A monopolist, on the other hand, will produce at a level based on its marginal revenue and marginal cost, rather than on consumers' demand. Therefore, the monopolist will charge a higher price and produce a lower quantity than is achieved in a competitive market. *Resources are under-allocated towards a monopolist's output, therefore monopoly power is a market failure.*

Chapter 6 Costs of Production

Costs of production in the short-run
- The law of diminishing returns
- Total, average and marginal product
- Total, average and marginal cost
- Explicit and implicit costs

Costs of production in the long run
- Economies of scale
- The relationship between SR ATC and LR ATC

Revenues
- Total, average and marginal revenue

Profit
- Normal profit
- Economic profit
- Profit maximization rule

Introduction to Costs of Production
Firms in a market economy are the providers of the goods and services that households demand in the product market. The incentive that drives firms to provide households with products is that of profit maximization.

Profit maximization: The goal of most firms is to maximize their profits. To do so, they must produce at a level of output at which the difference between their revenues and their costs is maximized.

$$Economic\ Profit = Total\ Revenue\ (TR) - Total\ Cost\ (TC)$$

To determine whether it will earn a profit at a particular level of output, a firm must, therefore, consider two economic variables: its costs and its revenues

Economic Costs: These are the explicit money payments a firm makes to resources owners for the use of land, labor and capital:
- Includes variable costs (payments for those resources which vary with the level of output)
- And fixed costs (payments for those resources which do not vary in quantity with the level of output),
- As well as the opportunity cost of the business owner

$$Total\ Cost = Variable\ Costs + Fixed\ Costs$$

Economic Revenues: This is the money income a firm earns from the sale of its products to households. At a particular level of output, a firm's total revenue equals the price of its product times the quantity sold.

$$Total\ Revenue = Price \times Quantity$$

Short-run versus Long-run Costs of Production

When examining a firm's costs, we must consider two periods of time.

- *The short-run:* The period of time in which firms can vary only the amount of labor and the raw materials it uses in its production. Capital and land resources are fixed, and cannot be varied.

  ➢ Example: When the demand for American automobiles fell in the late 2000s, Ford and General Motors responded in the short-run by reducing the size of their workforces.

- *The long run:* The period of time over which firms can vary the quantities of all resources they use in production. The quantities of labor, capital and land resources can all be varied in the long run.

  ➢ Example: When demand for American automobiles remained weak for over two years, Ford and General Motors began closing factories and selling off their capital equipment to foreign car manufacturers.

Variable costs and fixed costs: A firm's variable costs are those that change in the short-run as the firm changes its level of output. Fixed costs, on the other hand, remain constant as output varies in the short-run.

In the long run, all costs are variable, since all resources can be varied...

Short-run Costs of Production

The primary determinant of a firm's short-run production costs is the productivity of its short-run variable resources (primarily the labor the firm employs).

Productivity: The output produced per unit of input

- The greater the average product of variable resources, the lower the average costs of production in the short-run
- The lower the productivity of the variable resource, the higher the average costs of production
- Since in the short-run, only labor and raw materials can be varied in quantity, *LABOR IS THE PRIMARY VARIABLE RESOURCE...*

Labor productivity in the short-run: As different amounts of labor are added to a fixed amount of capital, the productivity of labor will vary based on *the law of diminishing returns*, which states...

The Law of Diminishing Returns: As more and more of a variable resource (usually labor) is added to fixed resources (capital and land) towards production, the marginal product of the variable resource will increase until a certain point, beyond which marginal product declines.

Productivity in the Short-run
The productivity of labor is the primary determinant of a firm's short-run production costs. The table below presents some of the key measures of productivity we must consider when determining short-run costs.

Productivity: The amount of output attributable to a unit of input.	
Examples of productivity:	"Better training has increased the productivity of workers" "The new robot is more productive than older versions" "Adding fertilizer has increased the productivity of farmland"
Total product (TP)	TP is the total output of a particular firm at a particular period of time. Example of TP: "After hiring more workers the firm's total product increased."
Marginal product of labor (MP_L)	$MP_L = \Delta TP/(\Delta Q_L)$ is the change in total product divided by the change in the quantity of labor
Average product of labor (AP_L)	$AP_L = TP/Q_L$ is the output per worker, or the total product divided by the quantity of labor employed

Productivity in the Short-run
Assume a bakery with three ovens wishes to start making bread. To do so, it must hire workers. How many workers should the bakery hire? That depends on the productivity of the labor as more workers are added to the three ovens.

Quantity of labor (Q_L)	Total Product	Marginal Product	Average Product
0	0	-	-
1	4	4	4
2	9	5	4.5
3	15	6	5
4	20	5	5
5	24	4	4.8
6	26	2	4.33
7	26	0	3.7
8	24	-2	3

The table presents a realistic estimate of the productivity of labor in the short-run
- Total product increases as more workers are hired, UNTIL the 6th worker, then total product remains flat and begins decreasing with the 8th worker hired.

- Marginal product (the output contributed by the last worker hired) increases until the 4th worker, and then marginal product begins decreasing.
- Average product (the output per worker) increases until the marginal product becomes lower than AP (at the 5th worker) and then begins decreasing.
- The productivity of labor is at its greatest at around 3 or 4 workers, which means the bakery's average costs will be minimized when employing approximately 4 workers.

The data from our productivity table can be plotted in a graph, with the quantity of labor on the horizontal axis and the total, marginal and average product on the vertical axis.

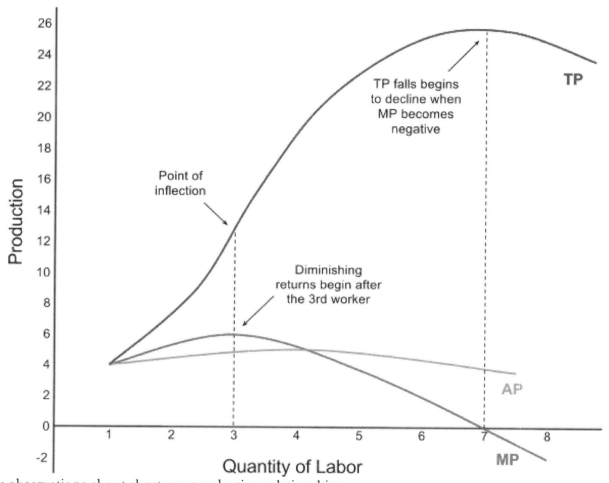

Key observations about short-run production relationships:
- The MP is the rate of change in the TP. As MP is increasing, TP becomes steeper, but when MP decreases, TP becomes flatter. When MP becomes negative, TP begins decreasing.
- MP intersects AP at its highest point. Whenever MP>AP, AP is increasing, but when MP<AP, AP is decreasing.
- The bakery begins experiencing *diminishing marginal returns* (the output of additional workers begins decreasing) after the third worker

If we look more closely at just the marginal product and average product curves, we can learn more about the relationship between these two production variables.

Explanation for diminishing returns:

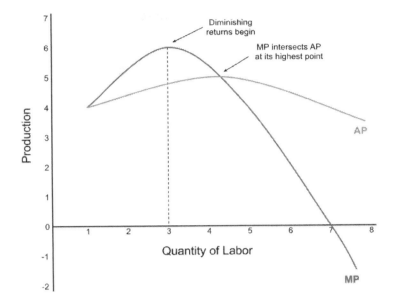

- With only three ovens in the bakery, the output attributable to the 4th – 8th worker becomes less and less.
- This is because there is *not enough capital to allow additional workers to continue to be more and more productive!*
- Up to the 5th worker, adding additional workers caused the *average product* to rise, since the marginal product was greater than the average.
- But beyond the 5th worker, diminishing returns was causing marginal product to fall at such a rate that it was pulling average output down with it. Worker productivity declines rapidly after four workers.
- A bakery wanting to minimize costs will not hire more than four workers.

Total Costs in the Short-run

A firm's costs in the short-run can be either fixed or variable. The table below presents some of the primary costs a firm faces, and indicates whether they are fixed costs or variable costs.

Resource costs in the short-run	
Fixed Costs in the short-run	**Rent** - the payment for land: Rent is fixed in the short-run since firms cannot add this resource to production. Rents must be paid regardless of the level of the firm's output.
	Interest - the payment for capital: Interest is fixed in the short-run since firms cannot add this resource to production. Interest must be paid on loans regardless of the level of the firm's output.
	Normal profit - the minimum level of profit needed just to keep an entrepreneur operating in his current market. If he does not earn normal profit, an entrepreneur will direct his skills towards another market. Normal profit is a cost because if a firm does not earn normal profit, it is not covering its costs and may shut down.
Variable Costs in the short-run	**Wages** - the payment for labor: Wages are variable in the short-run, since firms can hire or fire workers to use existing land and capital resources. Wage costs increase when new workers are hired, and decrease when workers are laid off.
	Transportation costs: Firms pay lower transport costs at lower levels of output.
	Raw material costs: vary with the level of output
	Manufactured inputs: fewer parts are needed from suppliers when a firm lowers output.

A firm's total costs include the costs of labor (variable costs) and the costs of capital and land resources (fixed costs).

Total Costs in the Short-run
Total fixed costs (TFC): These are the costs a firm faces that do not vary with changes in short-run output. *Could include rent on factory space, interest on capital (already acquired).*
Total variable costs (TVC): These are the costs a firm faces which change with the level of output in the short-run. *Could include payment for raw materials, fuel, power, transportation services, wages for workers, etc....*
Total cost: TFC + TVC at each level of output

Observe in the graph to the right
- The firm pays total fixed costs of $100.
- Its TVC increases at a rate determined by the law of diminishing returns
- Its total cost equals its TFC + TVC

A firm's total costs include the costs of labor (variable costs) and the costs of capital and land resources (fixed costs).

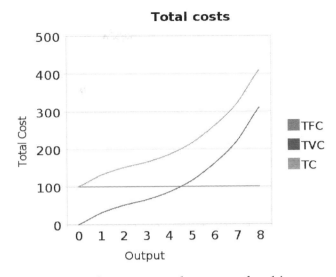

- *TFC:* Notice that regardless of the level of output, TFC remains constant. This is because these are costs that do not vary with output.
- *TVC:* Notice that when output is zero, TVC is zero, because you do not need to hire any workers or use any raw materials if you're not producing anything. As output increases, TVC continues to increase
- *TC:* Notice that when output is zero, TC = TFC. But once the factory begins pumping out products, TC rises with TVC. TC is the sum of TFC and TVC, since both fixed and variable costs make up total cost.

Diminishing Returns and the short-run costs of production:
- Notice that TC and TVC increase at a decreasing rate at first. This is when marginal product is increasing as more labor is employed (firms get "more for their money")
- However, beyond some point, costs begin to increase at an increasing rate. This is where diminishing returns set in and MP is decreasing. The firm is getting less additional output from each worker hired, but must pay the same wages regardless. (The firm gets "less for its money")

Per-unit Costs in the Short-run

Firms make decisions about their levels of output based not on total costs, rather on per-unit and marginal costs.

Per-unit Costs in the Short-run	
Average fixed cost: AFC=TFC/Q	AFC will decline as output rises, but it will never increase. This is because the fixed cost (which never goes up) is "spread out" as output increases. This is called "spreading the overhead"
Average variable cost: AVC = TVC/Q	For simplicity, we will assume that labor is the only variable input, the labor cost per unit of output is the AVC
Average total cost: ATC = TC/Q	Sometimes called unit cost or per unit cost. ATC also equals AFC + AVC
Marginal Cost: MC = ΔTVC/ΔQ	The additional cost of producing one more unit of output.

From Short-run Productivity to Short-run Costs

As worker productivity increases, firms get "more for their money", meaning per-unit and marginal cost decrease. When productivity decreases, costs increase.

The relationship between productivity and costs
- When productivity of its workers is rising, a firm's per unit costs are falling, since they're getting more output for each dollar spent on worker wages.
- When marginal product is increasing (increasing returns) marginal cost is falling. When average product is rising, average variable cost is falling.
- When MP and AP are maximized, MC and AVC are minimized
- When workers begin experiencing diminishing returns, MP falls and MC begins to rise.
- MP intersects average product at its highest point, and MC intersects average variable cost at its lowest point

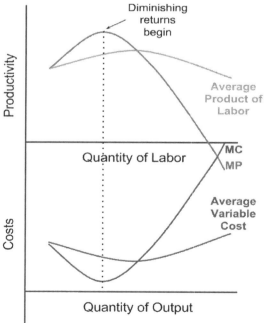

Graphing Per-unit Costs in the Short-run
The law of diminishing marginal returns dictates the relationships between a firm's short-run per unit costs

Short-run Cost Relationships	
ATC=AFC + AVC	The vertical distance between ATC and AVC equals the AFC at each level of output.
MC and ATC/AVC	MC intersects both AVC and ATC at their minimum. This is because if the last unit produced cost less than the average, then the average must be falling, and vice versa (just like your test scores!)
MC and diminishing returns	MC is at its minimum when MP is at its maximum, because beyond that point diminishing returns sets in and the firm starts getting less for its money!

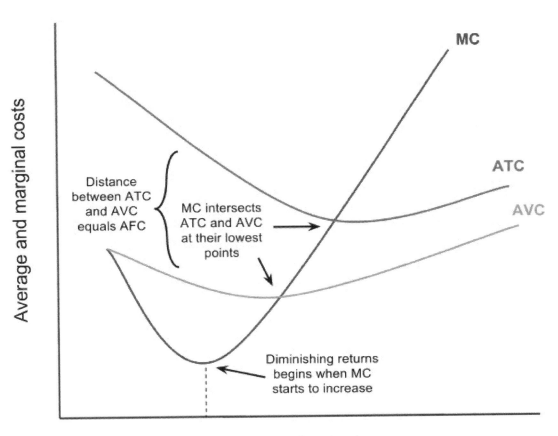

Costs of Production in the Long run

Long-run is the variable plant period, meaning that firms can open up new plants, add capital to existing plants, or close plans and remove capital if need be.

- Because capital and land are variable in the long run, the law of diminishing returns no longer applies.
- A firm's long-run average costs depend on how productivity of land, labor and capital change as a firm's output increases in the *variable plant-period.*
- As a firm's output increases in the long run, the firm's ATC will initially decrease, but eventually increase, based on the following concepts…

Three ranges of a firm's long-run Average Total Cost curve
Increasing Returns to Scale (Economies of scale): When a firm receives increasing amounts of output per additional unit of inputs (land, labor and capital). Average costs decrease as output increases. *Explanations: better specialization, division of labor, bulk buying, lower interest on loans, lower per unit transport costs, larger and more efficient machines, etc...*
Constant Returns to Scale: When a firm receives the same amount of output per additional unit of input. Average costs do not change as output increases.
Decreasing Returns to Scale (Diseconomies of Scale): When a firm becomes *"too big for its own good"*. The output per unit of input decreases as more inputs are added. Average costs increase as output increases. *Explanations: Control and communications problems, trying to coordinate production across a wide geographic may make firm less efficient.*

The concept of *economies of scale* explains why a firm adding new plants and capital equipment to its production will become more efficient as it expands.

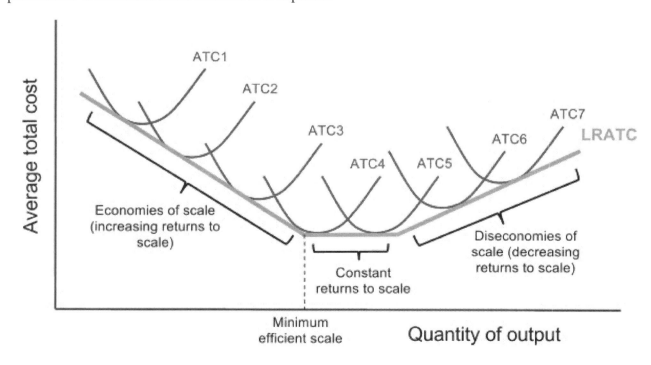

Examine the long-run average total cost curve in the graph on the previous page
- The small curves represent the short-run ATC curves experienced as the firm opens several factories in the long run (from 1 to 7 factories).
- As the firm opens its first 4 factories, its ATC continuously decreases. The firm is becoming *more efficient* in its production.
- With the 5th factory, the firm is no longer experiencing *increasing returns*, and instead has experienced *constant returns to scale*.
- With the 6th and 7th factories, the firm's ATC is rising, indicating it is becoming *less efficient*. The firm is experiencing *decreasing returns to scale*.

As a firm increases its output in the long run (the variable plant period), it at first becomes more and more efficient, but eventually inefficiencies cause its ATC to rise, as the firm gets "too big for its own good"

Costs of Production in the Long-run – Economies of Scale
Economies of scale arise due to several factors:
- Better prices for raw materials such as plastic and rubber parts for the toys due to larger bulk orders made by the firm as it grows.
- Lower costs due to higher quality and more technologically advanced machinery operating in larger factories.
- Lower average shipping and transportation costs as the firm produces and ships larger quantities of toys to the market when operating four factories than when operating only one.
- More favorable interest rates from banks for new capital as the firm becomes larger and therefore more "credit worthy".
- More bargaining power with labor unions for lower wages as the firm employers larger numbers of factory workers.
- Improved manufacturing techniques and more highly specialized labor, capital and managerial expertise.

Diseconomies of scale: When a firm becomes too big to manage efficiently, it becomes less efficient and average costs rise, making the firm less and less competitive. The best thing a firm experiencing diseconomies of scale can do is reduce its size or break into smaller firms.

Revenues
Costs are only half the calculation a firm must make when determining its level of economic profits. A firm must also consider its revenues.

Revenues are the income the firm earns from the sale of its good.
- *Total Revenue* = the price the good is selling for X the quantity sold
- *Average Revenue* = The firm's total revenue divided by the quantity sold, or simply the price of the good
- *Marginal Revenue* = the change in total revenue resulting from an increase in output of one unit

Market Structure and Price Determination:
- For some firms, the price it can sell additional units of output for never changes. These firms are known as "price-takers", and sell their output in highly competitive markets

- For other firms, the price must be lowered to sell additional units of output. These firms are known as "price-makers" and have significant market power, selling their products in markets with less competition.

Revenues for a Perfect Competitor
A firm selling it product in a perfectly competitive market is a "price-taker". This means the firm can sell as much output as it wants at the equilibrium price determined by the market.
- The marginal revenue the firm faces, therefore, is equal to the price determined in the market.
- The average revenue is also the price in the market.
- The MR=AR=P line for a perfectly competitive firm also represents the demand for the individual firm's product. Because a perfectly competitive seller is one of hundreds of firms selling an identical product, the firm cannot raise its price above that determined by the market.

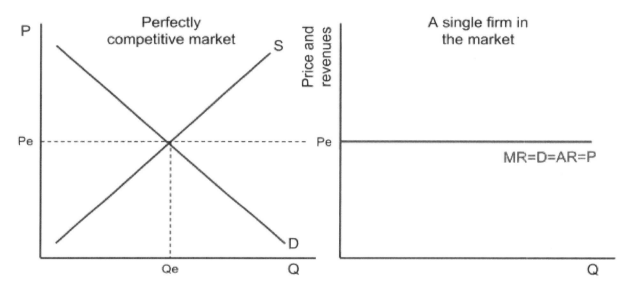

Demand for the perfectly competitive firm's output:
- Demand is perfectly elastic
- The firm has no price-making power.
- The price in the market equals the firm's marginal revenue and average revenue

Revenues for an Imperfect Competitor
A firm with a large share of the total sales in a particular market is a "price-maker", because to sell more output, it must lower its prices. For this reason…
- The marginal revenue the firm faces is less than the price at each level of output.
- The average revenue is also the price in the market.
- Because a firm with market power is selling a unique or differentiated product, it faces a downward sloping demand curve.

Consider the data in the table below, which shows the price, total revenue and marginal revenue for an imperfectly competitive firm:

Quantity of output (Q)	Price (P) = Average Revenue (AR)	Total Revenue (TR)	Marginal Revenue (MR)
0	450	0	-
1	400	400	400
2	350	700	300
3	300	900	200
4	250	1000	100
5	200	1000	0
6	150	900	-100
7	100	700	-200
8	50	400	-300

Revenues for an Imperfect Competitor

The firm whose revenues are depicted above will see the following Demand, Average Revenue, Marginal Revenue and Total Revenue:

Points to notice about the imperfect competitor:
- To sell more output, this firm must lower its price
- As it sells more output, its MR falls faster than the price, so the MR curve is always below the Demand curve (except at an output of 1 unit, when MR=P)
- The firm's total revenues rise as its output increases, until the 6th unit, when the firm's MR has become negative. MR is the change in TR, so when MR is negative, TR begins to fall.
- The firm would never want to sell more than 5 units. This would cause the firm's costs to rise while its revenues fall, meaning the firm's profits would be shrinking.
- The demand curve has a n elastic range and an inelastic range, based on the *total revenue test of elasticity*

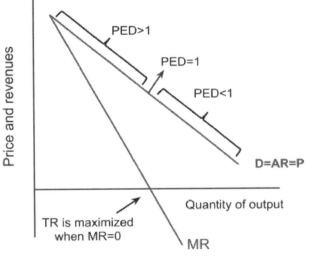

The Profit Maximization Rule

Considering its costs and revenues, a firm must decide how much output it should produce to maximize its economic profits.
- *Economic Profits = Total Revenues – Total Costs*
- *Per-unit Profit = Average Revenue (or price) – Average Total Cost*

The Profit-Maximization Rule: To maximize its total economic profits, a firm should produce at the level of output at which its marginal revenue equals its marginal cost
- For a perfect competitor, the P=MR, so the profit-maximizing firm should produce where its MC=P.
- For an imperfect competitor, the P>MR, so the profit-maximizing firm will produce at a quantity where its MC=MR.

Rationale for the MC=MR Rule: If a firm is producing at a point where its MR>MC, the firm's total profits will rise if it continues to increase its output, since the additional revenue earned will exceed the additional costs. If a firm is producing at a point where MC>MR, the firm should reduce its output because the additional costs of the last units exceed the additional revenue.

When MC=MR, the firm's total profits are maximized

Consider the firms below.
- The competitive, price-taking firm on the left will produce where its MC=MR, at a quantity of 6 units and at the market price of $50.
- The firm on the right, a price-making monopolist, will produce a lower quantity and sell at a higher price.

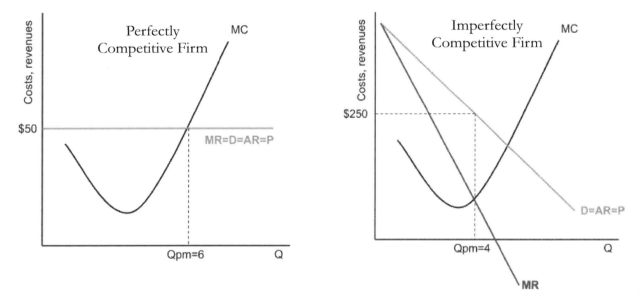

> **Normal profit:** the minimum level of profit needed just to keep an entrepreneur operating in his current market. If he does not earn normal profit, an entrepreneur will direct his skills towards another market.

> **Economic profit:** also called "abnormal profits". When revenues exceed all costs and normal profit. Firms are attracted to industries where economic profits are being earned.

Chapter 7 – Perfect Competition

Assumptions of the Perfectly Competitive Model
- Large number of sellers
- Homogeneous product
- No entry barriers
- Perfect information

Profit Maximization in the Short-run
- Produce where MC=MR
- If P>ATC, short-run economic profits can be earned

Profit Maximization in the Long run
- Easy entry and exit assure firms will only earn normal profits in the long-run

The Shutdown Rule
- When a firm should shut down while earning losses
- If total losses are greater than a firm's total fixed costs

Efficiency under Perfect Competition
- Allocative efficiency: Does the price equal the marginal cost?
- Productive efficiency: Do firms produce at their minimum ATC?

Introduction to Market Structures

Product markets come in many forms. The four market structures are introduced below.

Characteristic	Pure (or Perfect) Competition	Monopolistic Competition	Oligopoly	Monopoly
Number of Firms	VERY large number of firms	Fairly large number of firms	A few large firms dominate an industry	Only ONE firm. The firm IS the industry
Price making abilities of individual firms	Each firm is so small that changes in its own output do not affect market price, i.e. firms are price takers	Firms are small relative to the industry, meaning changes in one firms output have only a slight impact on market price	A change in one firm's output has significant impact on the market price, firms are price-makers.	Changes in the firm's output cause changes in the price, i.e. the firm is a price-maker!
Type of product	Firms all produce identical products, with no differentiation	Products are slightly differentiated. Firms will advertise to try and further differentiate product. Branding! Advertising!	Products can be identical (such as oil) or differentiated (such as Macs and Dells) Firms will likely use advertising to try and differentiate their products from competitors'	Unique product, no other firm makes anything like it.
Entry barriers	Completely free entry and exit from the industry, i.e. NO barriers to entry.	Limited barriers to entry, firms can enter or leave easily	There are significant barriers to entry	Significant barriers to entry exist, preventing new firms from entering and competing with the monopolist

Assumptions of the Perfectly Competitive Market Model
To begin our studies of competition in different markets, we will examine the perfectly competitive market model.

A perfectly competitive market is one in which:
- There is a very large number of firms,
- Selling identical products to one another,
- In which there are no barriers to entry or exit
- And in which individual firms have no control over the market price.

Example: Imagine you live in New York City and want to have a cheese pizza for lunch. Let's assume…
- There are hundreds of pizza shops in New York
- Every one of them has cheese pizza on their menu
- They all pay their workers minimum wage. They all buy cheese, dough and tomato sauce at the same prices
- It is cheap and easy to open a pizza shop, just as it is to shut one down if needed.

Based on these characteristics, the market for cheese pizzas in New York is close to perfectly competitive. You will pay the same price no matter where you order your pizza!

Perfectly Competitive Firms are "Price Takers"
An individual firm in a perfectly competitive market has no control over the price of its own output. This is because the price is determined based on *market supply* and *market demand*.

Note from the graph below that:
- The demand seen by the firm is determined by the price in the market.
- Price also determines the firm's marginal revenue
- The firm has no "price-making power" because if it raises its price, it will sell no output, and
- If it lowers its price, it will not be able to cover its costs of production.
- Demand for the individual firm's output is perfectly elastic
- To maximize its profits, a firm should produce where its marginal revenue equals its marginal costs.

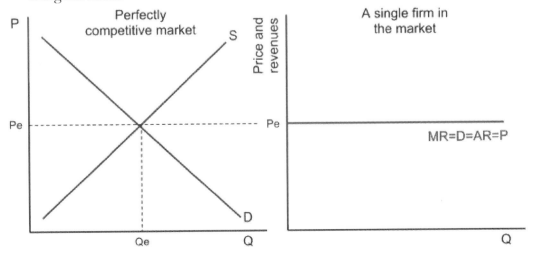

Profit Maximization for the Perfect Competitor
In our previous unit we learned that, to maximize its economic profits at any given time, a firm should produce at the quantity at which its marginal revenue (MR) equals its marginal cost (MC)

In the graph below:
- The firm is facing marginal revenue equal to Pe, determined by the market price at any given time.
- The firm's marginal cost increases steadily due to diminishing returns (to make more pizzas in the short-run, more cooks must be hired, but because capital is fixed the marginal product of cooks decreases as more are added)
- Based on its MC and MR, the firm will maximize its profits (or minimize its losses) by producing at Qf

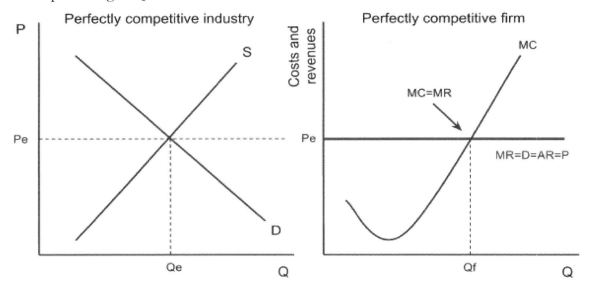

Determining Short-run Economic Profits or Loss
A firm will maximize its profits (or minimize its losses) by producing at the quantity where MR=MC. To determine whether a firm is actually earning profits, breaking even, or earning losses at this quantity, we must consider both the firm's average revenue (the price) and its average total cost.

Short-run Costs of Production: Recall from our earlier unit that a firm faces the following short-run production costs:
- Marginal Cost, which slopes upwards because of diminishing marginal returns
- Average variable cost, which is the per unit labor costs of production

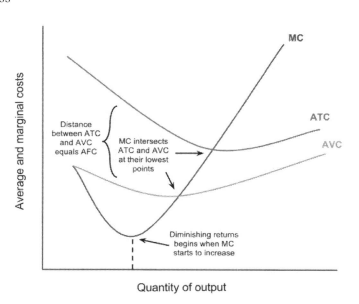

- Average total cost, which is the average variable costs plus the average fixed costs (the per-unit costs of fixed capital resources)
- Recall also that MC must intersect the average cost curves at their lowest points.

Profit Maximization in the Short-run: The Profit-earning Firm

If, when producing at its MC=MR point, a firm in a perfectly competitive market is selling its output for a price that is greater than its average total cost, then the firm is earning economic profits. Economic profits mean the firm is covering all of its explicit and implicit costs, and is earning additional revenue beyond these as well.

Study the graph below and note:
- The market demand is relatively high, presenting firms with a price that is greater than their ATC
- The firm's economic profits are represented by the shaded rectangle (P-ATC)xQ.
- The firm is maximizing its profits by producing where MR=MC.
- Due to the absence of entry barriers, these profits will not be sustained in the long run, as new firms will enter the market.

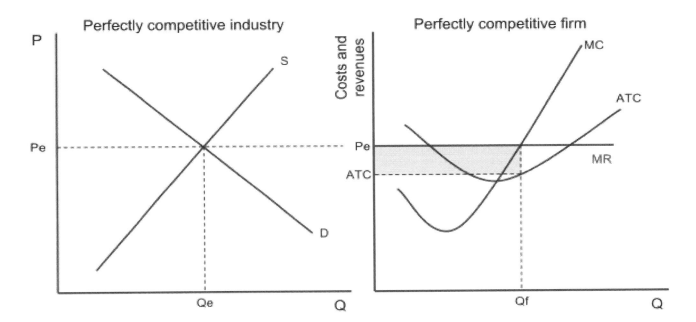

Profit Maximization in the Short-run: The Loss-minimizing Firm

If, when producing at its MC=MR point, a firm in a perfectly competitive market is selling at a price that is lower than its average total cost, the firm will be minimizing its losses, but earning no economic profit at all. The loss-minimizing firm will either exit the industry in the long run, or hope other firms exit until the supply decreases, causing the price to rise once again.

Study the graph below and note:
- The market demand is relatively low, so the price the firm can sell its output for is below its average total cost
- The firm's economic losses are the shaded area (ATC-P)xQ.

- The firm is minimizing its losses by producing where MR=MC.
- Due to the absence of entry barriers, these losses will be eliminated in the long run as firms exit the industry to avoid further losses.

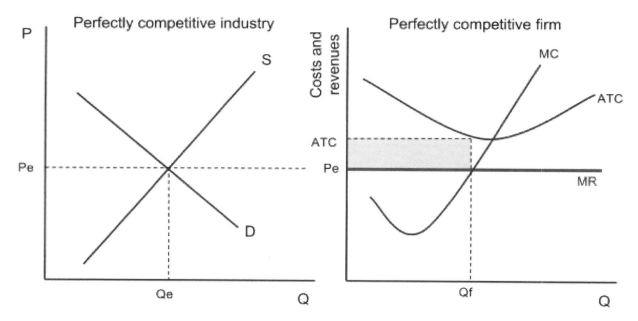

Profit Maximization in the Short-run: The Breaking-even Firm

If, when producing at its MC=MR level of output, the price the firm can sell its output for is exactly equal to the firm's minimum average total cost, then the best the firm can hope to do is to break even. Breaking even means a firm is covering all of its explicit and implicit costs, but earning no *additional* profit. The firm is earning only a **_NORMAL PROFIT._**

Study the graph below and note:

- The market demand and supply have set a price equal to the firm's minimum average total cost.
- The firm is just covering all its costs, meaning it is earning zero economic profits, but no losses
- If the firm produced at any quantity other than Qf, it would earn economic losses. By producing at Qf, it is breaking even.
- There is no incentive for firms to enter or exit this market.

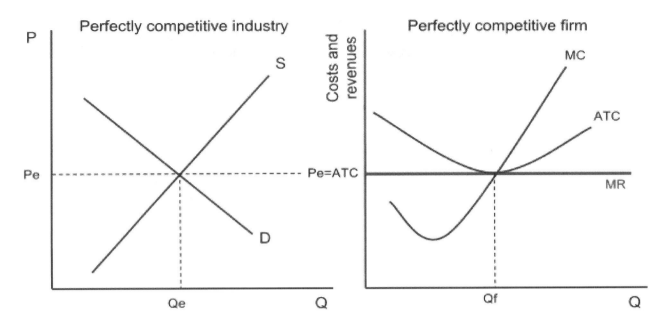

Profit Maximization in the Long run

Recall from an earlier unit that the long run is defined as: The period of time over which firms can adjust their plant size in response to changes in the level of demand for their product. New firms can enter a market and existing firms can exit a market in the long run. The long run is the variable-plant period.

Entry and exit in the long run: In perfectly competitive markets, firms can enter or exit the market in the long run.

- If economic profits are being earned, firms will be attracted to the profits and will want to enter the market
- If economic losses are being earned, some firms will wish to minimize their losses by shutting down and leaving the market
- Due to the entry and exit of firms in perfectly competitive markets, economic profits and losses will be eliminated in the long run and firms will only BREAK EVEN.

When all the firms in a perfectly competitive market are breaking even, a market is in its long-run equilibrium state. No firms will wish to enter OR exit a market in which firms are breaking even!

Profit Maximization in the Long run – Entry Eliminates Profits

When individual firms are earning economic profits in a perfectly competitive market, new firms will be attracted to the market, leading to an increase in market supply and a fall in the price.

Consider the pizza market on the next page:

- At the current level of demand and supply, the price ($20) per pizza is greater than the typical firm's ATC ($16).
- Pizza shops are making 200 pizzas each at a profit of $4 per pizza for a total profit of $800.
- Due to the low entry barriers, sellers of other products will be attracted to the pizza market, where easy profits can be earned.

87

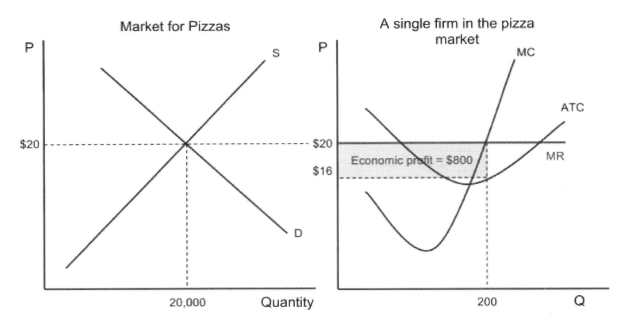

The existence of economic profits will attract new sellers to the pizza market.
- The number of sellers is a determinant of supply, so the market supply will increase
- The increased competition in the pizza market causes the price of pizzas to fall and the market quantity to increase

For the individual firm in the market:
- The price of pizza falls from $20 to $15.
- MR falls, causing the firm to reduce its output to maintain its MR=MC level
- Economic profit is eliminated, as the price falls to the firm's minimum ATC
- The firm's output is reduced as it now faces more competition
- *The market is in equilibrium again when the individual firm is only breaking even*

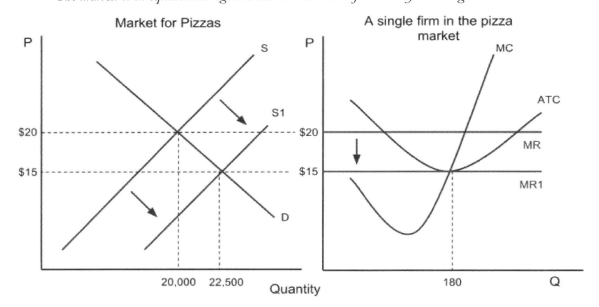

Profit Maximization in the Long-run – Exit Eliminates Losses

When individual firms are earning losses in a perfectly competitive market, certain firms will choose to leave the market to avoid losses and to seek profits elsewhere.

Consider the pizza market:
- At the current level of demand and supply the market price ($12) is lower than the typical firm's ATC ($16)
- Pizza shops are making 180 pizzas each at a loss of $4 per pizza, for a total loss of $720
- Due to the fact that it is easy to exit the market, some pizza shops will chose to shut down and seek profits elsewhere.

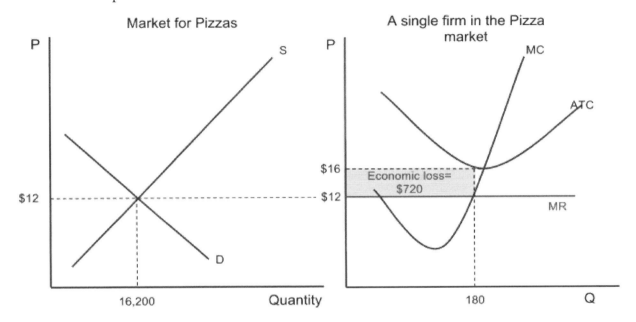

The experience of earning losses will make some firms wish to leave the market
- The number of sellers is a determinant of supply, so the market supply will decrease
- The decreased competition in the pizza market causes the price of pizzas to rise and the market quantity to decrease

For the individual firm that remains in the market:
- The price of pizza rises from $12 to $15
- MR rises, causing the firm to increase its output to maintain its MR=MC level
- Losses are eliminated, as the price rises to the firm's minimum ATC
- The firm's output increases as it now faces less competition
- *The market is in equilibrium again when the individual firm is only breaking even*

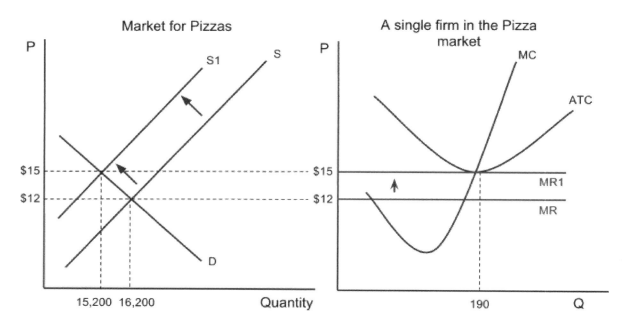

Long-run Equilibrium in Perfect Competition

A perfectly competitive market is in its long-run equilibrium ONLY when the typical firm is breaking even.

- Equilibrium is defined as *"a state of balance"*
- If any profits or losses are being earned, a PC market is out of balance, and firms will enter or exit the market until equilibrium is restored.

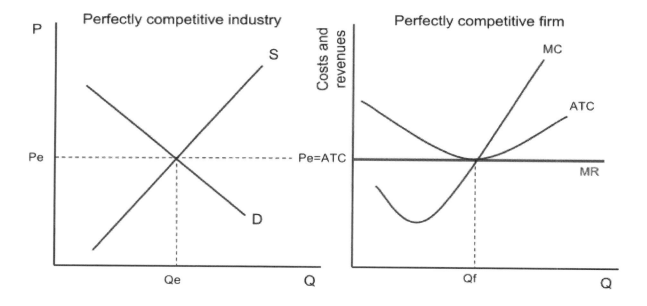

The Shut-down Rule

So far we have said that "if losses are being earned, some firms will exit the market until the remaining firms are breaking even once again". But this raises the question: *Which firms will exit the market, and which firms will stay?*

Revisiting our assumptions about perfect competition: Recall that we said that PC firms face identical costs of production. That is not 100% true, because one cost, the level of *normal profit,* can vary from seller to seller, even in perfect competition.

Normal profit is the implicit, subjective value of each business owner's skills and time. Some business owners will value their efforts more highly than others, even when all the other costs faced are identical to all other business owners' costs.
- For this reason, some sellers will be willing to tolerate greater losses for longer periods of time than other sellers.
- In other words, among firms facing identical *explicit costs* (wages, interests, rents), some will shut down sooner when earning losses than others due to their different levels of *implicit costs* (normal profit)

A firm facing economic losses has two choices:
1. Continue to operate your business, and hope that your average revenue (price) is at least high enough to cover your average variable costs (these are your operating costs in the short-run... you have to earn enough to pay your workers, at least!), OR...
2. Shut down and give up your fixed costs, which are those that must be paid EVEN if you shut your business down. A firm's loss when it shuts down is its total fixed costs, those payments to owners of capital and land resources (rent for your landlord, interest owed to the bank on money you borrowed to buy capital).

These tradeoffs give business owners a clear rule for WHEN TO SHUT DOWN:

If the price of your product is lower than a firm's average variable cost
or...
If the firm's total losses when continuing to operate are greater than its total fixed costs

If either of these criteria are true, then a firm *can always minimize its losses by shutting down and leaving the market.* If neither is true, the firm should remain in the market and continue to produce, and hope that the price rises again in the future.

A firm facing losses must compare its level of losses by continuing to operate to its level of losses if it shuts down.
- Total losses if it continues to operate = $(AR\text{-}ATC)\times Q$
- Total losses if it shuts down = $(ATC\text{-}AVC)\times Q$

Consider the Pizza Market:
- The demand for pizzas is so low that the price ($10) is lower than the firm's AVC ($11). The firm cannot even afford to pay its workers.
- The firm's total losses (17-10)x160, are greater than its total fixed costs (17-11)x160. The firm would minimize its losses by shutting down
- This firm should exit the market

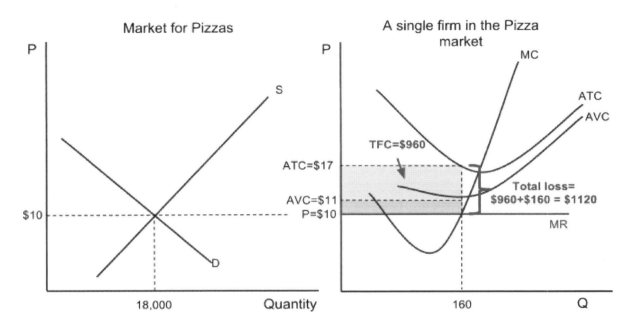

Efficiency in Perfectly Competitive Markets

In long-run equilibrium, purely competitive firms will produce the *efficient level of output and price*. Efficiency in economics is measured in two ways: Firms can be *productively efficient* and an industry can be *allocatively efficient*.

Productive Efficiency is achieve if firms produce at their *minimum average total cost:*
- Interpretation: *Firms are using resources to their maximum efficiency by producing their output at the lowest possible average total cost. Competition forces firms to use resources as efficiently as possible.*

Allocative Efficiency is achieved if a market produces at the quantity where marginal benefit equals marginal cost (where Price = Marginal Cost)
- Interpretation: *The right amount of output is being produced. There is neither under nor over-allocation of resources towards a good in a purely competitive industry.*
  - ➢ If the price were higher than the marginal cost, this is a signal that marginal benefit exceeds marginal cost and more output is desired,
  - ➢ If price were lower than marginal cost, the signal from buyers to sellers is that marginal cost exceeds marginal benefit and less output is desired.
  - ➢ Only when P = MC is the right amount of output being produced.

Productive Efficiency

Price acts as a signal in competitive markets of the demands (and therefore the marginal benefit) of consumers. Price will always equal firms' minimum ATC in the long-run, assuring that perfectly competitive sellers will be productively efficient.

- If price is high enough that firms are earning profits, then the signal from buyers to sellers is *WE WANT MORE*
- If price is low enough that firms are earning losses, then the signal from buyers to sellers is *WE WANT LESS*

Consider the market and firm here:

- Price is higher than the firm's ATC.
- The firm's are earning economic profits
- The signal from buyers is "we want more", so more firms will enter the market to satisfy demand.
- As new firms enter, price will fall to minimum ATC, and firms will be *more **productively efficient!***

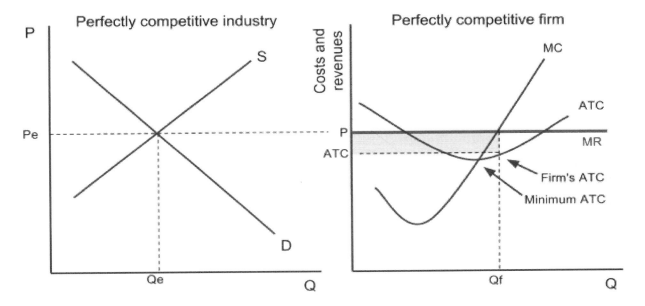

Study the graphs here:

- Assume the firm (which represents *all firms in this market*) produces at Q1.
- Market quantity supplied will be only Qs. At Qs, the demand (MB) is greater than the supply (MC) of the good. *Resources are under-allocated.*
- The profit-maximizing firm will increase its production to Qf to achieve the MR=MC point.
- As all firms do so, market quantity increases to Qe.
- *When all firms produce where P=MC, the shortage that existed at Qs is eliminated and resources are efficiently allocated toward this good!*

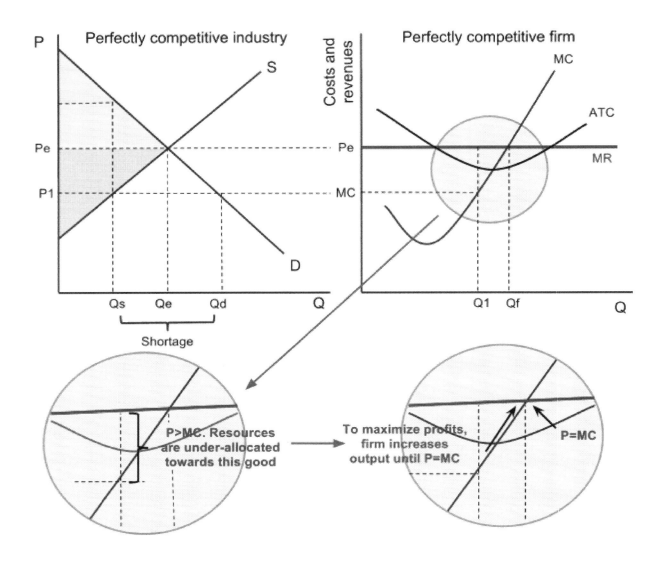

Chapter 8 – Pure Monopoly

Assumptions of the Pure Monopoly Model
- A single seller
- No close substitutes
- Significant entry barriers

Barriers to entry
- Economies of scale
- Branding
- Legal barriers

Revenue Curves
- The relationship between demand, average revenue and marginal revenue
- Why a monopolist will not operate in the inelastic portion of its demand curve
- Revenue maximization

Profit Maximization
- A monopolist will produce where MR=MC to maximize profits
- Barriers to entry permit firm to earn profits in the long-run

Natural Monopoly
- Economies of scale and natural monopoly
- Examples of natural monopolies
- Policies to regulate natural monopolies

Efficiency in Monopoly
- Monopoly power leads to inefficiency and welfare loss

Price Discrimination
- Necessary conditions for it to occur
- Effect on consumer and producer surplus and total welfare
- Effect on efficiency

Introduction to Pure Monopoly
In our last unit we studied perfect competition; next we move on to the opposite end of the competitive spectrum to pure monopoly. Monopolistic markets differ from perfectly competitive markets in nearly all characteristics. Study the table below to compare the two market structures.

Characteristic	Pure (or Perfect) Competition	Pure Monopoly
Number of Firms	VERY large number of firms	Only ONE firm. The firm IS the industry
Price making abilities of individual firms	Each firm is so small that changes in its own output do not affect market price, i.e. firms are price takers	Changes in the firm's output cause changes in the price, i.e. the firm is a price-maker!
Type of product	Firms all produce identical products, with no differentiation	Unique product, no other firm makes anything like it.
Entry barriers	Completely free entry and exit from the industry, i.e. NO barriers to entry.	Significant barriers to entry exist, preventing new firms from entering and competing with the monopolist
Efficiency	Will achieve both allocative and productive efficiency in the long-run	Will achieve neither allocative nor productive efficiency in the long-run

Pure monopoly is a market structure in which there is only ONE dominant firm that sells a unique product, has price-making power and in which there are significant barriers to entry.

Monopoly in the real world: Monopolistic markets are, in fact, more common than perfectly competitive markets. Quite a few of the goods and services we consume are provided by pure monopolies or at least NEAR monopolies:
- Microsoft: has a near monopoly in the market for PC operating systems, in which its Windows software runs on nearly every PC computer in the world.
- Local utilities: Most of us have only one option from where we buy our electricity, water, garbage collection, and gas. Most public utilities are provided by monopolists
- State liquor stores: In many US states liquor is sold in purely monopolistic state-run (or regulated) stores
- Cable and phone providers: Until the last decade or two, most people had only one option from where to buy their cable TV or their phone service. The adoption of cellular phone technology has made the phone service industry more competitive recently.
- Rail transportation: In the US, Switzerland, and many other countries, there is a purely monopolistic provider of train service in the country. If you want to travel by train across the US, you will travel on Amtrak.

Barriers to Entry in Monopolistic Markets
One characteristic ALL monopolies share is that there are significant barriers to entry, which keep competition out of the market. It is these entry barriers that protect a monopolist's power. *Without high entry barriers, new firms would enter the market and reduce the price-making and profit-making power of the monopolist.*

Examples of entry barriers:
- Legal barriers: Monopolists may have exclusive rights granted by the government to provide a certain good or service. Other legal barriers may include patents or copyrights held by the firm that prevent competition from producing a similar product.
- Economies of Scale: The "advantages of being big". Some firms have achieved such a great size that they can simply produce their good more efficiently, and thus sell it for a lower price, than any other firm could hope to do, keeping competition out of the market.
- Ownership of resources: If a firm has exclusive access to the resources needed to make its good, then no other competitor can hope to begin producing the good. An example of this is the global diamond giant De Beers, which has exclusive access to over 80% of the known diamond mines in the world.
- Strategic pricing: A monopolist may be able to block entry to the market by temporarily selling its output at a price below its per-unit costs (and earning short-run losses). This deters competitors from entering
- Brand loyalty: If a firm has a brand that is well known and popular among consumers, then other firms will find it hard to get a foothold in the market, allowing the monopolist to maintain market share.

Revenue Curves for the Pure Monopolist
Demand, average revenue and marginal revenue as seen by the monopolist are quite different as that seen by the perfectly competitive firm.
- Recall that in perfect competition, Demand, MR, and AR as seen by the firm is a horizontal line equal to the equilibrium price determined in the market.
- In monopoly, the demand seen by the firm IS the market demand, and MR falls faster than demand, AR and price. Study the table below to see why.

Q (thousands)	P (AR)	TR (PxQ) thousands	MR ($\Delta TR/\Delta Q$) thousands
0	55	0	-
1	50	50	50
2	45	90	40
3	40	120	30
4	35	140	20
5	30	150	10
6	25	150	0

Assume the data represents the sales and revenues of tickets to an amusement park (the only one in town):
- At $55, no tickets will be sold. At $50, 1,000 will be sold. In order to sell more tickets, the park must lower prices. *The park is a price-maker!*
- The park's revenues rise until it has sold 5,000 tickets, then it peaks at $150,000.
- MR falls as output increases, but it falls twice as rapidly as the price.
- Graphically, the MR will be below the demand curve.

Revenue Curves for the Pure Monopolist
Because the monopolist must lower its price to sell additional units, its marginal revenue of a particular unit will always be lower than the price that unit sells for (except at an output of 1).

Points about the monopolist's demand:
- Demand for the firm's output IS the market demand
- When MR is positive, demand is elastic (since TR increases when P decreases)
- If this firm wanted to sell more tickets, it would have to keep lowering the price and MR would become negative.
- When MR is negative, demand is inelastic, since a decrease in P will cause TR to fall.

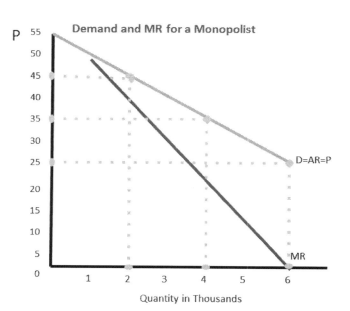

Q (thousands)	P (AR)	TR	MR
0	55	0	-
1	50	50	50
2	45	90	40
3	40	120	30
4	35	140	20
5	30	150	10
6	25	150	0

PED and the Monopolist's Demand
Examine the graph to the right. Notice that the monopolist's demand can be seen to have:

- An elastic range (where MR is positive)
- An inelastic range (where MR is negative)
- At Q_{RM} the monopolist's total revenue is maximized

A monopolist will NEVER produce in the inelastic range of its demand! Because if a monopolist were to sell beyond Q_{RM} it would always do better by decreasing its output until MR were positive once again.

- Total costs would decrease as the firm reduces its output
- Total revenue would increase, therefore…
- Reducing output to a point below Q_{RM} would definitely increase the firm's profits (remember, economic profits = TR-TC)

Notice that if a monopolist wished to maximize its revenues, it would produce at the quantity where MR=0!

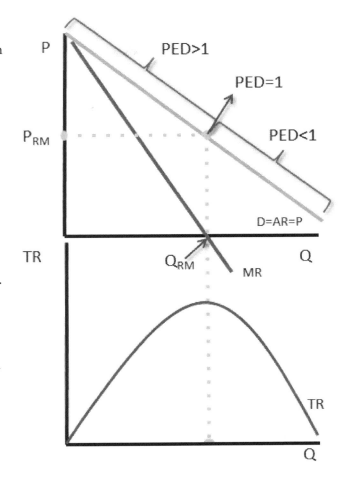

The Profit Maximizing Monopolist
Just like a firm in perfect competition, a monopolist wishing to maximize its profits wants to produce at the quantity at which:

Marginal Revenue = Marginal Cost

To determine a monopolist's profit maximizing level of output, therefore, we must consider both its revenues and its costs.

Notice in the graph:

- The monopolist's MC and ATC demonstrate the same relationships as a firm in perfect competition.
- The firm will produce at the quantity at which MC=MR to maximize profits.

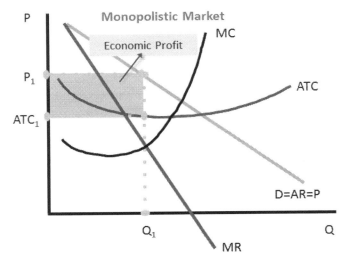

- Subtracting the firm's ATC at Q1 from the price it can sell Q1 units of output for, and multiplying by the quantity produced find the area of economic profit. Economic profits = (P-ATC) x Q.
- Because of the entry barriers in this market, the firm's profits ARE sustainable in the long-run

The Loss Minimizing Monopolist
Having monopoly power does not guarantee that a firm will earn economic profits.

- If demand for a monopolist's output falls, or
- If the monopolist's costs of production rise, then…
- The firm can go from earning economic profits to earning losses.

To minimize losses, a monopolist should produce at its MR=MC level of output.

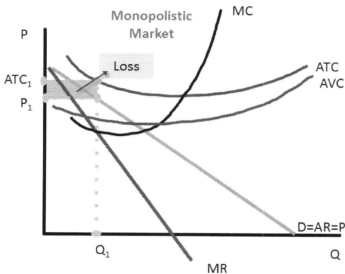

Notice in the graph:
- The firm is producing at its MR=MC level of output, but at this point the firm's ATC is greater than the price it can sell for.
- The firm is earning economic losses represented by the triangle.
- Despite its losses, this firm should NOT SHUT DOWN, because the price still covers the average variable cost; this firm can continue to operate in the short-run.
- Only if total losses were larger than the total fixed costs should the firm shut down.
- To reduce or eliminate its losses, the firm must try and increase demand or reduce its costs.

The Breaking-even Monopolist
Of course, it is also conceivable that a monopolist will be selling its product at a price that is exactly equal to its ATC. This would mean that the monopolist is *breaking even*.

Notice in the graph:
- The firm is producing at its MR=MC level of output. At this point the firm's ATC is exactly equal to its price.
- The firm's total revenues are exactly equal to its total costs.
- The firm is covering all of its explicit and implicit costs,

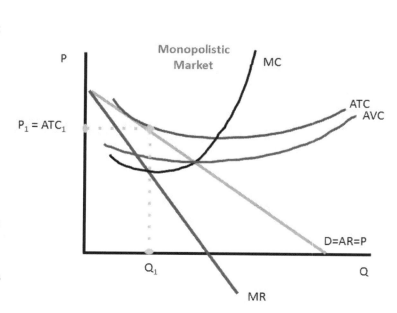

meaning it's earning a *normal profit*, but it is not earning any *economic profit*.
- If the firm wishes to earn economic profits, it will have to improve or advertise its product to increase demand or increase the efficiency with which it uses resources to reduce its costs.

When a Monopolist should Shut Down
Recall from the previous chapter that firms should follow a simple rule when deciding whether or not to shut down and leave a market:
- If the price it can sell for is lower than the firm's average variable cost, or…
- If total losses are greater than the firm's total fixed costs.

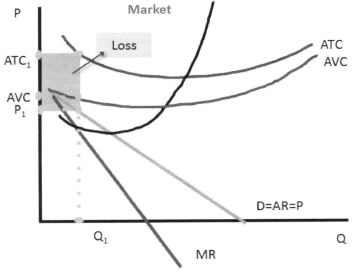

Notice in the graph:
- The firm is producing at its MR=MC level of output, but at this point the price the firm can sell its output for is lower than the firm's average variable cost.
- This firm cannot even afford to pay its workers for each unit they produce (the per-unit labor costs are higher than the price)
- The gray rectangle represents the firm's losses (ATC-P) x Q. The firm's total fixed costs, (ATC-AVC) x Q, are smaller than the total losses. This means that if the firm shuts down it will minimize its losses

Long-run Equilibrium in a Monopolistic Market
In our study of perfect competition we learned the following:

In Perfectly Competitive Markets
- If firms are earning economic profits in the short-run, new firms will enter the market, increasing the supply, reducing the price and eliminating profits.
- If firms are earning economic losses in the short-run, some firms will exit the market, reducing the supply, increasing the price and eliminating losses for the firms that remain.
- In the long-run, firms in perfectly competitive markets will only break even.

However, in Monopolistic Markets:
- If the firm is earning economic profits in the short-run, those profits will be maintained as long as the firm can keep demand for its goods high and its costs low, *because entry to a monopolistic market is blocked!*
- If the firm is earning economic losses in the short-run, those losses will be maintained as long as the firm cannot increase the demand for its product or reduce its price. *Exit from a monopoly market is difficult because of the large economies of scale that often characterize large, single sellers.*

Natural Monopoly

Not all industries that are monopolies necessarily *need to be monopolies*. In other words, sometimes firms have monopoly power for legal or technical reasons:

- If a firm has an exclusive permit from the government to provide a particular good
- If a firm has "cornered the market" for a particular resource needed to produce the good
- If a firm has priced competitors out of the market using predatory pricing strategies…
- Any of these sources of monopoly power could be considered economically *inefficient and therefore undesirable* to some extent.

However, there is a type of monopolistic industry in which the dominance of a single firm is economically justifiable and actually beneficial for society! It is called a natural monopoly

Natural Monopoly: When a single producer can do the production of a good more efficiently than could possibly be accomplished by multiple producers, an industry is a natural monopoly.

- This typically occurs in industries in which there are significant economies of scale.
- If the total demand for a good intersects the firm's ATC while the firm is still achieving *increasing returns to scale*, then having multiple firms produce the good cannot be more efficient than having a single producer and seller.

Natural monopolies typically occur in industries with huge economies of scale, such as utility industries or those for good that require significant capital investments to produce, and for which there is a relatively small demand in total.

Assume, for example:

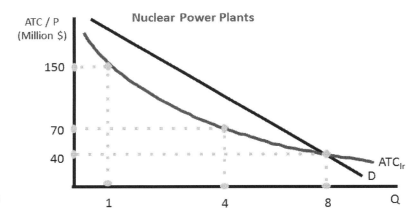

- France wishes to build 8 new nuclear power plants. The government must decide whether to hire one firm to build all 8 plants (which would give that firm a monopoly), or
- Hire 2 plants to build four plants each, or
- Hire 8 firms to build one plant each

Based on the Long-run ATC curve, which represents the per-plant costs of the firms in the industry, we can observe the following:

- It would cost one firm a total of **$320m** [8x40] to build eight plants
- It would cost two firms a total of **$560m** [2(4x70)] to build eight plants
- It would cost 8 small firms a total of **$1,200m** [8(150)] to build eight plants

Based on our analysis above, we calculated the following options for France:

- Hire 8 firms to build nuclear plants at a total cost of $1,200 million
- Hire 4 firms at a total cost of $560 million, or

- Hire 1 firm at a total cost of $320 million

The *least-cost* way to build power plants is to allow a single firm to build all eight plants. The firm will be better able to achieve *economies of scale* and build the plants at a lower average cost than if eight separate firms were competing with one another for the resources needed to build the plants.

This industry is a natural monopoly, because costs are minimized, and thus the price of the electricity the plants produce can be kept lower as well, when only a single firm produces the good in question.

Natural Monopoly and the need for Government Regulation:

A monopoly in a key industry like electricity generation can potentially be very harmful for consumers of the product being produced. Monopolists tend to charge a price that is higher, and produce a quantity that is lower than what is socially optimal.

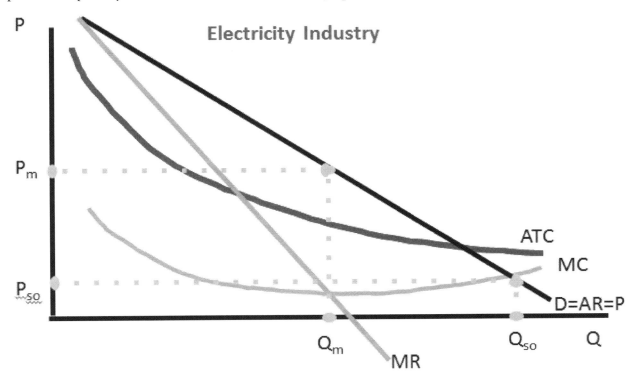

Assume the market for electricity is a natural monopoly:
- To maximize its profits, the electricity company will produce where MC=MR, at a quantity of Qm, and charge a price of Pm
- The socially optimal quantity (where P=MC) is Qso. This is the *allocatively efficient* level of output, at a price of Pso.
- Unregulated, the industry will under-produce electricity and charge a higher price, leaving many households unable to afford this important product.

To ensure a more socially optimal level of output and price, government regulation is needed. Either subsidies or price ceilings (or both) will increase output and reduce price.

To ensure that a naturally monopolistic industry produces at a level closer to the *allocatively efficient* price and quantity (where P=MC), either subsidies or price controls should be imposed by the government.

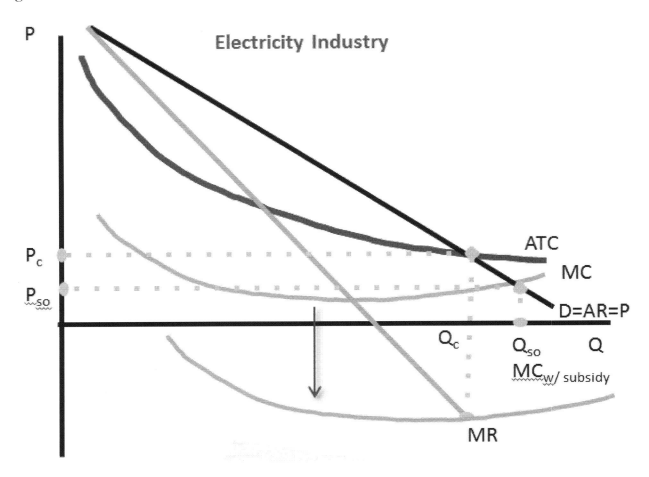

Regulations to increase output and decrease price of a natural monopoly:
- A price ceiling of Pso is below the firm's ATC, so the firm will be earning economic losses and will shut down in the long-run. This is *not a good regulation.*
- A price ceiling of Pc, which is equal to the firm's average total cost, will increase the firm's level of output (to Qc) and lead a price closer to Pso. The firm will break even, and earn a *fair return* for its services. *This is a commonly used regulation*
- A subsidy that reduces the firm's MC will lead to the firm producing more electricity and lowering its price. *Subsidizing natural monopolists is a commonly used regulation.*

Efficiency under Pure Monopoly
As we learned in the previous unit, perfectly competitive industries are both *allocatively* and *productively efficient.* This is because, in the long-run:
- *Price will always equal marginal cost (the allocatively efficient level of output)*
- *Firms will always produce at their minimum ATC (the productively efficient level of output)*

To determine whether monopolies are efficient, we must consider whether the same conditions are met

Allocative Efficiency: Consider the two industries below:

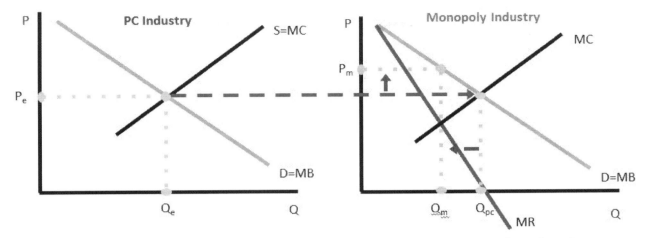

- Price and output in perfect competition are determined by market supply and market demand.
- Output occurs at the P=MC point, meaning resources are *efficiently allocated* towards the product
- The firm's MR and MC determine Price and output in monopoly.
- At Qm, P>MC, indicating that resources are *under-allocated* towards the produced

Under perfect competition, firms are forced to be productively efficient, meaning they produce their products at the lowest possible average total cost. Without competition, however, monopolists are NOT productively efficient.

Productive efficiency: Consider the two firms:

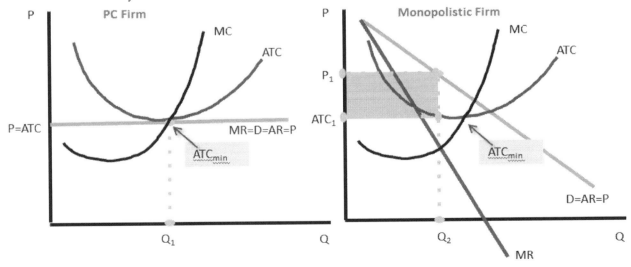

- The PC firm produces at Q1, where its ATC is at its minimum.
- The PC firm is productively efficient, because at any other point it would be earning losses and would have to exit the market

- The monopolist produces at Q2, where its ATC is higher than its minimum.
- The monopolist is NOT productively efficient. Without competitors, it is able to use resources in a less efficient way, and is not forced to sell at a price as low as its minimum ATC.

As compared to perfect competition, monopolistic markets have several observable effects

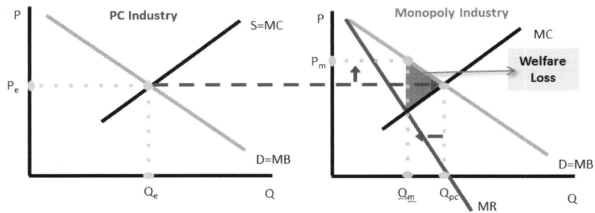

Effects of monopoly on price, output and efficiency·
Higher price
Lower output
P > min. ATC: Productive inefficiency
P > MC: Allocative inefficiency *(resources are under-allocated towards the product)*
Efficiency Loss (Welfare loss) occurs
There is a loss of Consumer surplus in exchange for higher firm profit. Welfare loss results
Income transfer: consumers pay a higher price, shareholders of the monopoly enjoy higher profits.

Some other effects of an industry becoming a monopoly include:
- Economies of scale: Some monopolized industries have only one firm because economies of scale exist over such a wide range of output. It is possible that one or two large firms can achieve a lower ATC than many smaller firms. This is called a *natural monopoly*.
- Simultaneous consumption: One product can satisfy a large number of consumers at the same time. Example: Microsoft Windows. Marginal Cost for Microsoft is essentially nothing, so ATC_{LR} declines over the entire range of output.
- Network effect: describes the phenomenon of a product's value increasing the more users it has. Examples: cell phones, the internet, email, Facebook! Tends to move markets towards monopoly as more and more consumers flock to a product because of the "network" that develops around it.

- Income Transfer: Consumer surplus is lost because of higher price. Firm profits are higher b/c of market power. Compared to PC industries, monopolies represent a transfer of income from consumers to shareholders in the monopolistic firm.

Price Discrimination

One benefit a firm with monopoly power may enjoy is the *ability to charge different prices to different consumers for the same product*. This is known as *price discrimination*.

Conditions: In order for a firm to be able to price discriminate, the following conditions must be met:
1. *The firm must have some monopoly power:* A perfect competitor could not possibly charge different prices to different consumers, because there are hundreds of other firms selling the same good for the low market price.
2. *Market Segregation:* In order to price discriminate, the seller must be able to determine who is willing to pay what. The firm must segregate the market by age, gender, race, nationality, income level, or some other method that distinguishes between consumers willing to pay more for a good and those willing to pay less
3. *No Resale:* If a buyer who paid a low price is able to sell the product to someone who the seller wants to charge a high price to, the seller's monopoly power is undermined and it becomes difficult to price discriminate. So it must be difficult or impossible for buyers to resell the product to one another.

Price discrimination comes in many forms, or *degrees*.

First Degree – by individual consumer: This is the most difficult type of price discrimination for firms to practice. It requires the firm to determine *exactly what each consumer is willing and able to pay for the product, and charges each consumer that price*. This type leads to the greatest profits for the firm, but leaves consumers with *no consumer surplus. Sometimes referred to as **perfect price discrimination**.

Second Degree - by quantity: A more common form of price discrimination in which the firm charges lower per-unit price to consumers who "buy in bulk". Consider a pack of toilet paper rolls with four rolls in it compared to a package with 24 rolls in it. Usually, if you buy the larger package, you will pay considerably less per roll. This is a form of price discrimination which charges higher prices to people who are not willing to buy in bulk.

Third Degree – by consumer group: Another common form of price discrimination; consumers may pay more or less for a good depending on their age, their gender, when they buy, the passport they carry, etc... Consider movie theater tickets (age), airline tickets (when you buy), haircuts (gender) and admission to museums or national parks in some countries (nationality).

There are countless examples of firms price discriminating. Here are a few:
- Movie theaters: Charge different prices based on age. Seniors and youth pay less since they tend to be more price sensitive.
- Gas stations: Gas stations will charge different prices in different neighborhoods based on relative demand and location.

- Grocery stores: Offer coupons to price sensitive consumers (people whose demand is inelastic won't bother to cut coupons, thus will pay more for the same products as price sensitive consumers who take the time to collect coupons).
- Quantity discounts: Grocery stores give discounts for bulk purchases by customers who are price sensitive (think "buy one gallon of milk, get a second gallon free"… the family of six is price sensitive and is likely to pay less per gallon than the dual income couple with no kids who would never buy two gallons of milk).
- Dell Computers: Dell price discriminates based on customer answers to questions during the online shopping process. Dell charges higher prices to large business and government agencies than to households and small businesses *for the exact same product!*
- Hotel room rates: Some hotels will charge less for customers who bother to ask about special room rates than to those who don't even bother to ask.
- Telephone plans: Some customers who ask their provider for special rates will find it incredibly easy to get better calling rates than if they don't bother to ask.
- Damaged goods discounts: When a company creates and sells two products that are essentially identical except one has fewer features and costs significantly less to capture more price-sensitive consumers.
- Book publishers: Some paperbacks cost more to manufacture but sell to consumers for significantly less than hard covers. Price sensitive consumers will buy the paperback while those with inelastic demand will pay more for the hard cover.
- Airline ticket prices: Weekend stopover discounts for leisure travelers mean business people, whose demand for flights is highly inelastic, but who will rarely stay over a weekend, pay far more for a round-trip ticket that departs and returns during the week.

The effects of price discrimination can be shown graphically, which allows us to determine whom benefits, which suffers, and whether it increases or decreases overall welfare and efficiency. The graphs below compare a single price monopolist and a *perfectly price discriminating firm.*

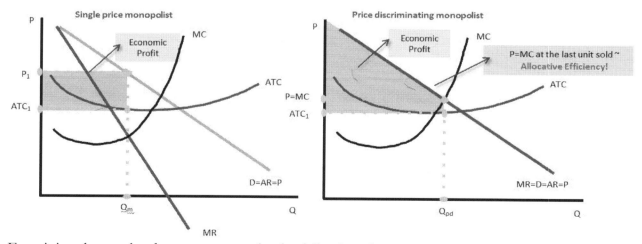

Examining the graphs above, we can make the following observations about price discrimination:

Effects of price discrimination:
- The price discriminating firm earns a greater level of economic profits than the single-price firm. The shaded triangle on the right is bigger than the shaded rectangle on the left

- More output is produced and sold due to price discrimination: Q_{pd} is greater than Q_m
- Consumer surplus is reduced (or eliminated in the case of perfect price discrimination). When every consumer pays exactly what she is willing to pay, no one has any "extra" happiness when buying the product.
- Allocative efficiency is improved! The higher level of output will be closer to (or equal to in the case of perfect price discrimination) the P=MC level. The firm will continue to sell right up to the point the last price it charged is equal to the firm's marginal cost.
- More efficient allocation of resources: Despite the fall in consumer surplus, overall welfare is actually improved by price discrimination. More people can afford the product than under a single price seller.

Chapter 9 - Monopolistic Competition and Oligopoly

Monopolistic Competition
- Assumptions of the model
- Revenue Curves
- Profit Maximization in the short-run
- Profit maximization in the long-run
- Non-price competition
- Monopolistic competition and efficiency
- Monopolistic competition compared with perfect competition and monopoly

Oligopoly
- Assumptions of the model
- Game Theory
- Open/formal collusion
- Tacit/informal collusion
- Non-collusive oligopoly and the kinked demand curve

Introduction to Monopolistic Competition

The third market structure we will study gets is name from sharing some characteristics with pure monopoly and some with perfect competition. Below are some of the key characteristics of this market structure:

Characteristic	Monopolistic Competition
Number of Firms	Fairly large number of firms, each with a relatively small amount of market share
Price making abilities of individual firms	Firms are small relative to the industry, meaning changes in one firms output have only a slight impact on market price. While they are price-makers, demand will be relatively elastic compared to a pure monopolist
Type of product	Products are slightly differentiated. Firms will advertise to try and further differentiate product. Branding and advertising are used to attempt to increase demand for the firm's product over competitors.
Entry barriers	Entry to and exit from the market is relatively easy. If profits exist, new firms will enter, if losses are earned, it can be expected that some firms will exit.
Efficiency	Because of their price-making power, firms will produce at a price that is higher than their marginal cost and higher then their minimum ATC, meaning the industry is not economically efficient.

Examples of Monopolistically Competitive Markets

Monopolist competition is probably *the most common market structure* in most market economies. The characteristics apply to a wide range of industries in which many sellers compete for the business of buyers. Examples include:

- Restaurants in a major city: There are hundreds of restaurants in a city of any reasonable size. They all sell a similar product (food), which is differentiated from one seller to the other (Chinese, Mexican, French, Barbecue, etc…) Each restaurant can set its own prices, but only to an extent (have you ever seen a $100 hamburger?)
- Apparel: The market for clothing is highly competitive, and like restaurants, the hundreds (or thousands) of clothing manufactures are competing for our business by differentiating their products from the competition. Again, firms have some price-making power, but consumers can always switch brands if prices rise too much, so demand is relatively elastic.
- Automobiles: Even the car market shows some characteristics of monopolistic competition, although due to the relatively substantial economies of scale, it could be considered oligopolistic in some markets. Each car is a close substitute for all other cars, but is differentiated to try to make demand for it less elastic.

Revenue Curves for the Monopolistic Competitor

Because each firm in in a monopolistically competitive market makes a product that is differentiated from its competitors, it is able to control the price for its output, *but only to a certain extent.*

Observations of the Monopolistic Competitor's Demand and MR curves:

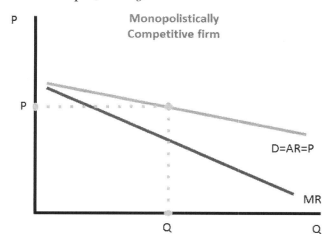

- With many other firms making similar products, each firm faces a relatively, but not perfectly, elastic demand curve.
  - ➤ A price increase will lead to a large loss of buyers, but a price decrease will lead to a large increase in buyers.
- In order to sell additional units of its product, a firm must lower the price of all its output.
  - ➤ For this reason, the firm's marginal revenue will fall faster than its price (see a mathematical explanation for this in the chapter on Monopoly.

Profit Maximization in the Short-run

As with firms competing in the other market structures, a monopolistic competitor will maximize its total profits when it produces at the quantity of output at which MR=MC

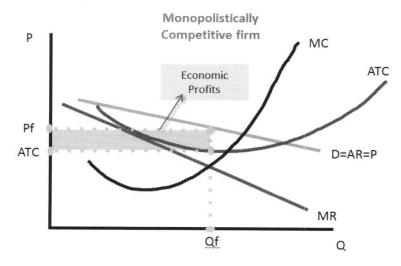

Observe from the graph:

- The firm is producing at its profit maximizing quantity (Qf) and charging the price consumers are willing to pay for that quantity (Pf)
- At this point, price is greater than ATC, so the firm is earning an economic profit.
- Given the existence of profits in this market (assuming this firm is a typical firm) new firms will be attracted to the industry.
- Since entry barriers are low, these short-run economic profits are likely to be eliminated in the long-run as new firms enter the market.

Profit Maximization in the Long-run – Entry Eliminates Profits

One of the key characteristics of monopolistic competition is the *low entry barriers.* Getting into such a market is relatively cheap and easy, and entrepreneurs will therefore be attracted to any economic profits that are earned.

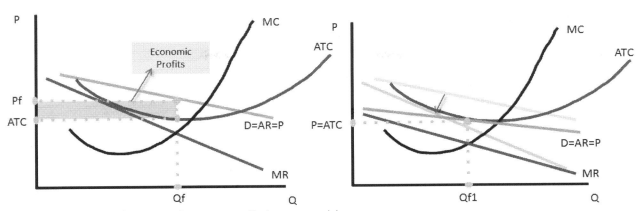

From short-run to long run in monopolistic competition:

- Economic profits attract new firms to the market, increasing the amount of competition and the number of substitutes for this firm's product
- More competition reduces demand for this firm's product, and makes it more elastic (flatter). Demand decreases until the firm is only breaking even

Profit Maximization in the Long-run – Exit Eliminates Losses

Just as it is relatively easy to enter a monopolistically competitive market, it is also easy to leave. This means that if the firms in such a market are earning losses, some will exit the market, increasing the demand for those that remain until they are breaking even.

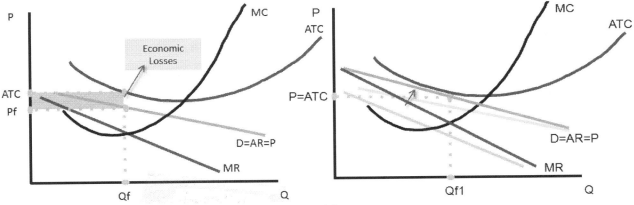

From short-run to long run in monopolistic competition:

- Due to weak demand, firms are earning losses, leading some firms to exit the market. As they do so, demand for the remaining firms increases...
- Less competition increases demand for this firm's product, and makes it less elastic (steeper). Demand increases until the firm is breaking even again

Monopolistic Competition in Long-run Equilibrium
Because of the low entry and exit barriers, firms in monopolistically competitive markets will *only break even in the long-run* (just like in perfect competition).

Non-price competition: Because firms face so much competition for their output, they will find it difficult to compete on price. In order to break even (or earn profits), a firm must compete through other, non-price means, including:

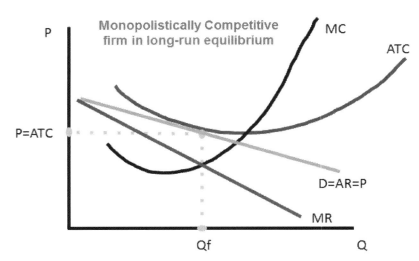

- Branding: By developing a recognizable brand image, firms attempt to build consumer loyalty, giving the firm more price-making power
- Product development: Continuously improving its product through research and development will keep demand high.
- Customer service: Offering good customer service and support may increase demand
- Location: Good access to large numbers of consumers allows a firm to charge higher prices
- Advertising: Making buyers aware of product features through advertising increases demand, giving the firm a greater chance of earning economic profits in the long-run

Efficiency in Monopolistically Competitive Markets
To determine whether monopolistically competitive firms are economically efficient, we must determine whether:

- $P = MC$: This is an indicator of allocative efficiency, since price represents the marginal benefits of consumers and MC the marginal cost to producers
- $P = minimum\ ATC$: This tells us whether firms are productively efficient, since if the price equals the lowest ATC, then firms are forced to use their resources in the *least-cost manner*.

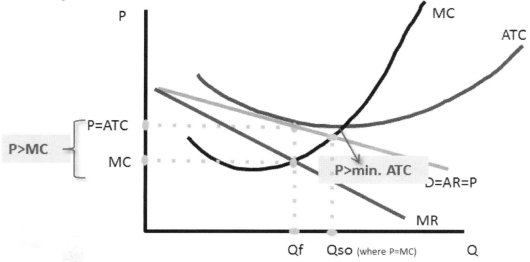

Efficiency is not achieved!
As we can see in the graph, a monopolistic competitor in long-run equilibrium will achieve neither productive nor allocative efficiency. The lack of competition allows firms to produce at a cost higher than their minimum ATC and produce a quantity lower than what is socially optimal.

Monopolistic Competition compared to Perfect Competition
It may appear that, since they do not achieve economic efficiency, monopolistically competitive markets are less desirable than perfectly competitive markets. However, there are also several benefits of monopolistic competition over perfect competition.

Characteristic	Perfect Competition	Monopolistic Competition
Price and Quantity	Price is low and quantity is high. Allocative and productive efficiency are achieved and consumer surplus is maximized as a result.	Price is higher and quantity lower than in perfect competition, neither type of efficiency is achieved and consumer surplus will be less.
Product Variety	Every firm sells an identical product. There is no variety for consumers to choose from.	Every firm differentiates its product, at least slightly, from every other seller, giving consumers a wide variety to choose from.
Profits	Firms will always break even in the long-run, and due to the high level of competition there is nothing an individual firm can due to earn profits, only an increase in market demand can lead to short-run profits	Firms have more ability to make profits through successful non-price competition and product differentiation, which if done well can earn a firm profits, even over time.

Introduction to Oligopoly
The final market structure we will study lies between monopolistic competition and pure monopoly on the competitive spectrum. Oligopolies are industries with a few large sellers, each with a substantial share of the total market demand.

Characteristic	Oligopoly
Number of Firms	A few large firms dominate the industry, each with a substantial share of total demand. There are few enough firms that in some cases, collusion is possible (when firm coordinate price and output decisions). Collusion can be: • Open / formal • Tacit / informal
Price making abilities of individual firms	A change in one firm's output has significant impact on the market price, firms are price-makers.
Type of product	Products can be identical (such as oil) or differentiated (such as Apple computers and PCs) Firms will likely use advertising to try and differentiate their products from competitors'
Entry barriers	There are significant barriers to entry, such as economies of scale, legal barriers, ownership of resources, etc…

Examples of Oligopolistic Markets
Oligopoly is a relatively common form of market structure. Many of the consumer goods and services we demand are provided by oligopolistic firms, including:
- Cell phone service providers: In most countries, consumers will have only a few choices for whom to buy their cell plan from. The providers all differentiate through options such as text messaging, data plans, call time, etc…
- Airplane manufactures: Boeing and Airbus are the two dominant firms in the market for jumbo-jets. The firms differentiate through fuel efficiency of their craft, number of seats, and so on.
- Movie studios: Only six big Hollywood studios make over 90% of the movies that make it to the big screen.
- Beer in the United States: Despite the fact that there are thousands of independent breweries in the US, only two large corporations produce 80% of the total beer supply. Both firms offer dozens, perhaps hundreds of varieties to try to differentiate their product from the competition
- Petrol for cars: Automobile fuel is a product often sold by a handful (a dozen or so) of large firms. Fuels, unlike the other products above, are a homogeneous product, so firms differentiate through location, primarily.

Collusion in Oligopolistic Markets – the Game Theory Model
Because there are only a few large firms in oligopolistic markets, they often have a strong incentive to cooperate, rather than compete, with one another on output and pricing decisions.

To understand why collusion is so attractive to oligopolistic firms, it is useful to think of competition between them as a sort of game. For this, we will use a model of oligopoly behavior known as game theory.

Game Theory: The study of strategic decision making through the use of games

Consider the following example: Two firms, Swisscom and Sunrise, provide cell phone service to consumers in Switzerland. These firm are trying to decide on the following:
- Whether to offer unlimited data to their customers (we will refer to this option as FREE), or
- Whether to charge customers based on data usage (we will refer to this option as PAY)

The profit of each firm depends not only on whether IT offers free data, but also on whether its competitor offers free data. In this regard, the firms are highly *interdependent* on one another

The possible levels of profit Sunrise and SwissCom can earn depending on their decision regarding data plans AND based on the competition's decision can be plotted in a table called a *payoff matrix*.

Study the payoff matrix below:

In this "game":
- Each firm can either choose "PAY" or "FREE"
- The number on the left in each box is the possible level of economic profit (in millions of Swiss francs) enjoyed by Sunrise.

Payoff Matrix		SwissCom	
		PAY	FREE
Sunrise	PAY	10 , 10	5 , 20
	FREE	20 , 5	7 , 7

- The number in the right in each box is the possible profit earned by Swisscom.
- Notice that each firm's profit depends largely on what the competition chooses to do.

Determining the likely outcome of the game:
Assume the firms do not collude. What will each firm most likely do? To determine the most likely outcome in the game below, consider the possible payoffs the firms face.

If Sunrise chooses "PAY"
- And SwissCom also chooses PAY, Sunrise will earn profits of 10 million
- But if SwissCom chooses FREE, Sunrise's profits will fall to 5 million
If Sunrises chooses "FREE"
- And SwissCom chooses PAY, Sunrise will earn profits of 20 million
- But if SwissCom also chooses FREE, Sunrise's profits will be 7 million.

Determining a dominant strategy:

A strategy is dominant if it results in a higher payoff regardless of what strategy the opponent chooses.

- In this game, both firms have a dominant strategy of choosing FREE.
- If SwissCom chooses PAY, Sunrise can do better by choosing FREE.
- If SwissCom chooses FREE, Sunrise can do better by choosing FREE.

Payoff Matrix		SwissCom	
		PAY	FREE
Sunrise	PAY	10 , 10	5 , 20
	FREE	20 , 5	7 , 7

Both firms can always do better by choosing to offer FREE data!

This game is known as the *Prisoner's Dilemma*. The firms in the game face a dilemma because:
- Both firms want to maximize their own profits, but…
- The rational thing to do is to offer FREE data, because the potential profits are so great!
  ➢ 20 million francs if the competitor chooses PAY, and
  ➢ 7 million francs if the competitor chooses FREE,
  ➢ For a total possible payoff of 27 million francs
- The possible payoffs for offering PAY are lower
  ➢ 10 million francs if the competitor offer PAY, and
  ➢ 5 million francs if the competitor offers FREE,
  ➢ For a total possible payoff of 15 million francs

When they act in their own rational *self-interest*, both firms end up earning *less profits* than if they had instead acted irrationally.

The dilemma is that, ultimately, the firms are likely to earn LESS total profits between them by offering FREE data than they would have earned if they had only chosen PAY data. This is because *collusion was not possible.*

BUT WHAT IF THE FIRMS WERE ABLE TO COLLUDE?

Game theory teaches us that in oligopolistic markets:
- Firms are highly interdependent on one another and that…
- There is a good reason for firms to collude with one another, because
- Through collusion, firms can choose a strategy that maximizes total profits between them, however…
- Such an outcome (both firms choosing PAY in our game) is highly *unstable,* because both firms have a strong incentive to cheat.

Game theory in the real world
This model of oligopoly behavior can be used to analyze the behavior of firms in oligopolistic markets on several levels, including:
- Whether to set a high price or a low price,
- Whether to advertise or not,
- Whether to offer free customer service
- Whether to offer a 1 year warranty or a three year warranty,
- Whether to open a store in a certain location or not... and so on...

In each of these scenarios, the decision one oligopolist makes will impact not only its own level of profits, but also those of its close competitors.

Collusion in Oligopolistic Markets – Forms of Collusion
Collusion is defined as the open or tacit cooperation between firms in an oligopolistic to set prices or agree on other strategies that often benefit the firms at the expense of consumers.

Open / Formal Collusion: The firms in a particular industry may form an official organization through which price and output decisions are agreed upon. This is called a *CARTEL*
- Cartels are illegal in most industries in most countries, due to their anti-competitive nature
- The firms in a cartel will choose an output and price that a monopolist would choose
- The price consumers pay will be higher, the output lower (consumer surplus lower)
- Cartels tend to stifle innovation among firms and reduce both productive and allocative efficiency.
- Due to the *prisoner's dilemma* explained earlier (there is always an incentive to cheat in a collusive oligopoly), cartel arrangements are often unstable and difficult to maintain. Once the majority of firms have agreed to a high price and reduced output, each individual firm has a strong incentive to increase its output to take advantage of the higher price in the market. If all firms do this, the market price will fall and the cartel will fail

Examples of cartels: OPEC (Organization of Petroleum Exporting Countries), International sugar producers, international coffee growers, drug cartels of Latin America.

Tacit / Informal Collusion: Since formal collusion is illegal in many countries, oligopolistic firms have devised way to collude informally. The most common form of tacit collusion is Price Leadership:
- Price leadership: This is when the biggest firm in an industry sets a price and the smaller firms follow suit. If the price leader raises its price, the competitors will too. If it lowers price, smaller firms will follow.
- Usually a *"dominant firm"* (typically the largest in the industry) establishes the price and smaller firms follow.
- Prices tend to be *"sticky"* upwards, since firms are hesitant to raise prices and lose market share to rivals.
- However, prices are *"slippery"* downwards, which means if one firm lowers its prices, others will follow suit so they don't lose all their business.

Price Wars: When tacit agreements break down, firms may engage in price wars, in which they continually lower their prices and increase output in order to try and attract more customers than their rivals.
- This can cause sudden increases in output and decreases in price, *temporarily approaching an efficient level.*
- Once firms realize low prices hurt everyone, price leadership is usually restored, and prices rise once more.

Non-Collusive Oligopolies – the Kinked Demand Curve Model
What if collusion is not possible? Price and output decisions in oligopolies can be analyzed using a more traditional model of firm behavior, the demand curve.

Consider the market for hamburgers: Assume there are only two firms selling hamburgers, McDonald's (the Big Mac) and Burger King (the Whopper).

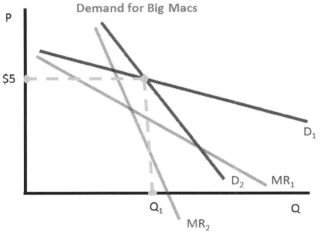

- The current price of both Big Macs and Whoppers is $5.
- McD's is considering changing its price.
- If McD's lowers its price, it should assume that BK will also lower its price, because if they do not, they will lose many consumers to McD's.
- With this assumption, demand for Big Macs is likely highly inelastic below $5 ($D_2$). Very few new customers will buy Big Macs, since the price of Whoppers will also fall.
- If McD's raises its price, it should assume that BK will ignore the price increase, since they know lots of Big Mac consumers will switch over to Whoppers.
- With this assumption, demand for Big Macs is highly elastic above $5 ($D_1$). Many Big Mac consumers will switch to Whoppers, since the price of Whoppers will stay at $5 when McD's raises its price

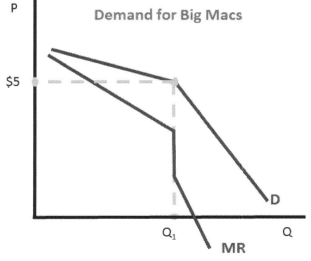

Based on the analysis above, we can conclude that the demand for Big Macs, as seen by McDonald's is actually a *kinked demand curve.*

Demand is highly elastic above the current price:
- BK will ignore a price increase by McD's
- Many consumers will switch to Whoppers
- A price increase would lead to a fall in McD's total revenues.

Demand is highly inelastic below the current price:
- BK will match price increases by McD's
- Very few new consumers will buy Big Macs
- A price decrease would lead to a fall in McD's total revenues

The price in a non-collusive oligopolistic market tends to be very stable. Firms are unlikely to raise or lower prices since in either case, total revenues will fall, possibly reducing profits.

Even as a firm's costs rise and fall, the firm is not likely to quickly change its level of output and price in a non-collusive oligopoly. Observe the graph below:

Assume due to rising beef prices, the marginal costs of Big Macs has risen from MC1 to MC3
- Following its profit maximization rule of producing where MC=MR, McD's should not change its price or quantity, even as the price of beef rises.
- Only if marginal cost rose higher than MC3 would McD's have to raise its price and reduce its output to maintain it profit maximizing level.
- Only if marginal cost fell lower than MC1 would McD's have to lower its price and increase its output to maintain profit maximization.

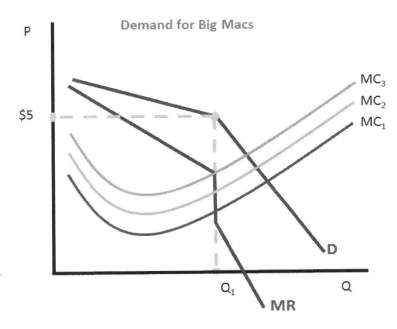

Prices and output are highly inflexible in a non-collusive oligopolistic market!

Chapter 10 – The Theory of Consumer Behavior
- Total Utility and Marginal Utility
- Utility Maximization – equalizing marginal utility per dollar spent on various goods
- Individual demand and market demand curves
- Income and substitution effects

Introduction to the Theory of Consumer Behavior
Throughout our study of Microeconomics we have examined the behaviors of firms competing in markets of varying levels of competition. We have learned:
- How firms decide the profit-maximizing level of output,
- How firms decide the revenue-maximizing level of output
- How firms know when they should shut down,
- When firms will wish to enter or exit a market

This can all be summarized as *firm behavior*. What we have not focus on yet is *Consumer Behavior*. In this unit we will examine the *THEORY OF CONSUMER BEHAVIOR:*

How rational consumers decide on the optimal combination of goods to consume with their limited budget in order to maximize their total utility at any given time.

Utility: In Economics, we refer to the welfare of consumers as *utility*. To allow us to measure the utility of consumers, we will refer to an imaginary value of happiness, called the *UTIL*. One UTIL equals one unit of happiness…

To introduce the theory of consumer behavior, it helps to think for a moment about your own behavior as a consumer…

Imagine you have $100 to spend this week. In the table below, identify
- 5 goods or services you would spend your money on.
- The approximate price of each product, and
- The quantity you would buy

Item	Price	Quantity

Questions:
1. How did you decide which items to put in your "basket"?
2. Is your basket identical to your classmates? Why or why not?
3. How would a change in the price of one of the items affect the quantity you buy?

4. How would a change in your budget affect the composition of your basket?

Chances are, every member of your class had entirely different goods in his or her table than you did. Precisely WHY every individual consumes a different "basket of goods" from every other individual in a market economy can be understood by the following:

- Every consumer behaves rationally: Consumers try to get the "most for their money" to maximize their total utility
- Every consumer has different preferences: Consumers have clear cut preferences and can determine how much marginal utility they get from consuming more units of a product
- Every consumer is under a budget constraint: All consumers face a budget constraint, therefore must make decisions about what they buy based on their limited budget
- Every product has a price: Every product has a price, so consumers must weigh their purchasing decisions based on their marginal utility from consumption and the price of the goods they consume

Total Utility and Marginal Utility
As explained in the introduction, rational consumers wish to maximize their happiness, or *utility* when buying goods and services. Otherwise, what is the point of spending money at all? Two concepts that will help us understand HOW consumers maximize utility, therefore, are:

- Total Utility (TU): This is the total happiness of a consumer at a particular level of consumption. Total utility will generally increase as total consumption of particular good increases, until the consumer has "had too much" of the good, when total utility will begin to decline.
- Marginal Utility (MU): This is the increase in total utility resulting from the consumption of *each additional unit* of a particular good.

$$MU = \Delta TU / \Delta Q$$

- Since MU measures the change in TU, as long as MU is positive at a particular level of output, TU will be increasing. But if MU becomes negative, TU will decrease.

The Law of Diminishing Marginal Utility
Recall from earlier units that demand for a particular good is *inversely related to the good's price*. One of the explanations for this relationship was *the law of diminishing marginal utility*, which states:

The greater the levels of consumption of a particular good, the less utility consumers derive from each additional unit of the good.

Consider the total and marginal utility one derives from consuming ice cream. Notice the following:

- The first scoop provides you with 5 utils, so TU = 5 at Q=1
- Additional scoops of ice cream provide you with *less and less additional happiness*. Nothing tastes quite as good as that first scoop! MU declines beyond the first scoop, but TU continues to increase, until…
- The fourth scoop: At four scoops your TU is maximized, but the 4th scoop provided you with no additional utility.
- Beyond four scoops, you've "had too much". TU begins decreasing while MU becomes negative.

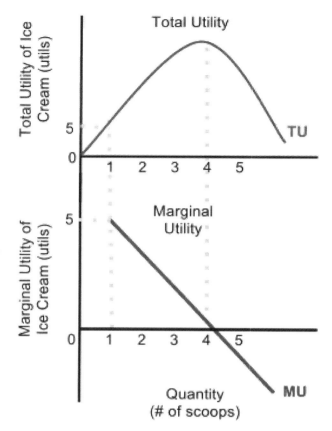

The Utility Maximization Rule

With the law of diminishing marginal utility in mind, we must now determine how a consumer should decide what to buy. Assume the following:

- You have a budget of $20 that you wish to spend entirely on two goods
- The two goods you are trying to decide between are Widgets (w) and Robotrons (r)
- The price of Widgets (Pw) is $5 and the price of Robotrons (Pr) is $2

To determine how many of each good you should buy, you must consider the utility each good provides. Consider the table below. First, calculate the MU at each level of consumption

Quantity	Widgets: Pw=$5		Robotrons: Pr=$2	
	TU	MU	TU	MU
1	10		5	
2	18		9	
3	24		12	
4	28		14	
5	30		15	

At first glance, it may appear that you should spend all your money on Widgets, because they clearly provide more total utility than Robotrons. But this would be a mistake, because Widgets also cost more than robotrons. Instead, there is a simple rule to follow to maximize utility:

The Utility Maximization Rule: To maximize your total utility, you should instead consume the combination of good that maximizes your marginal utility per dollar spent, so that:

$$MU_w/P_w = MU_r/P_r \ldots$$

and so on with other goods

With this rule in mind calculate the marginal utility per dollar spent on Widgets and Robotrons:

Quantity	Widgets: Pw=$5			Robotrons: Pr=$2		
	TU	MU	MU/P	TU	MU	MU/P
1	10	10		5	5	
2	18	8		9	4	
3	24	6		12	3	
4	28	5		14	2	
5	30	2		15	1	

Now we can study the table to determine how you should spend your $20 to maximize your total utility. Of course, if you had no budget constraint, you would consume 5 Widgets AND 5 Robotrons, but this would cost you $35, more than you have to spend. So choices must be made

Quantity	Widgets: Pw=$5			Robotrons: Pr=$2		
	TU	MU	MU/P	TU	MU	MU/P
1	10	10	2	5	5	2.5
2	18	8	1.6	9	4	2
3	24	6	1.2	12	3	1.5
4	28	4	0.8	14	2	1
5	30	2	0.4	15	1	0.5

At 2 widgets and 3 robotrons, you've maximized your total utility given your limited budget of $20, because the MU/P of each good is equal.

How to decide what to buy: The goal for consumers is to always maximize marginal utility per dollar.
- You should buy a Robotron first, giving you a MU/$ of 2.5. Remaining budget = $18
- Next you should buy a second Robotron, which gives you an MU/$ of 2. Remaining budget = $16
- Next you should buy a Widget, which gives you an MU/$ of 2. Remaining budget = $11

- A 2nd Widget will now give you an MU/$ of 1.6, compared to 1.5 for a 3rd Robotron. Remaining budget = $6
- A 3rd Robotron now gives you an MU/$ of 1.5, compared to 1.2 for a 3rd Widget: Remaining budget = $4
- Based on the utility maximization rule, you should buy 2 widgets and 3 robotrons, where MUw/Pw=MUr/Pr

Individual Demand and Market Demand

An individual consumer's marginal utility curve for a particular good represents that individual's demand for the good.

- If we consider demand as a signal of what a consumer is willing to pay for a good, and
- We recognize that what consumers are willing to pay is based on the utility they get from a good.

With this in mind, we can see a relationship between consumers' marginal utilities and market demand.

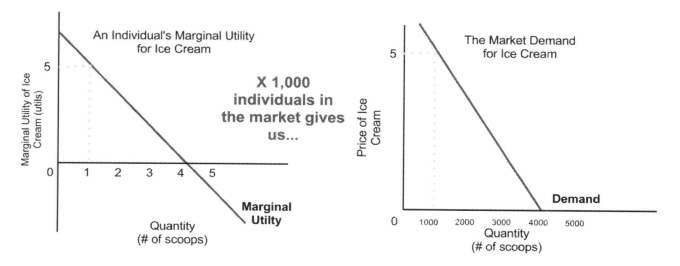

Consider the market for ice cream:
- Assume there are 1,000 consumers in the market,
- Each with a similar MU for ice cream.
- When we sum the individual MU curves for each consumer, we get the market demand for ice cream.
- For 1,000 scoops, consumers would pay $5, based on their high MU for the first scoop.
- To sell more ice cream, price must fall, based on consumers' diminishing marginal utility for ice cream.

Chapter 11 – Resource Markets

- Derived factor demand
- Marginal Revenue Product (MRP)
- Marginal Resource Cost (MRC)
- Profit maximization rule of resource employment (MRP=MRC)
- Perfectly competitive labor markets
- Monopsonistic labor markets
- The least-cost rule of resource employment

Introduction to Resource Markets

Throughout most of this course we have examined the interactions of buyers and sellers in *product market*, in which households are the buyers and firms the sellers. Recall from our circular flow model, however, that a market economy includes a market in which the roles are reversed.

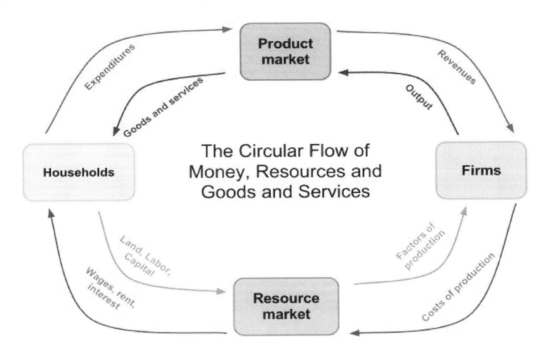

Resource (or Factor) Markets: Where households provide firms with the factors of production needed to produce good and services. The resources sold include: *Labor, Land and Capital.* Households receive money payments for their resources. These are:

- For Labor – WAGES
- For Land – RENT
- For Capital - INTEREST

These payments are determined just like any other price, by market supply and demand.

Degrees of Competition in Resource Markets

Resource markets, like product markets, can have lots of competition or be relatively uncompetitive. However, unlike product markets, competition in resource markets is among the BUYERS of resources, not among the SELLERS of products.

A perfectly competitive resource market: Is one in which there are hundreds of firms competing with one another to HIRE WORKERS… The market price is the wage rate firms pay workers, and this is determined entirely by the market demand for labor and the market supply of labor.

Firms in perfectly competitive labor markets are known as "wage-takers" because they can hire as many workers as they like at the equilibrium wage rate. They do not need to raise wage to attract more workers.

An imperfectly competitive resource market: Is one in which there is only one firm (or a relatively small number of firms) hiring all of one particular type of labor. This type of labor market is known as a monopsony, which means "single buyer"

Firms in a monopsonistic labor market are known as "wage-makers" because in order to attract more workers, they must raise the wages they pay all their workers.

Derived Resource Demand

Demand for any resource (labor, land or capital) is *derived demand*. This means it depends on other factors, including:

- The price of the good the resources is used to produce,
- The productivity of the resource

The demand for a resource is determined primarily by the productivity of the resource. Recall from an earlier unit the law of diminishing returns. This stated that;

As additional units of a variable resource put towards the production of a good using fixed resources, the output of additional units of the variable resource will eventually decrease.

- In other words, the more labor you add to a fixed amount of capital, the less additional output the labor will produce.
- For this reason, demand for labor is going to be inversely related to the price of labor (the wage rate).
- *Firms will only wish to hire more workers as the wage rate falls.*

Marginal Revenue Product

The demand for a resource (we will focus on labor) is based on the productivity of the resource and the price of the good being produced. Labor demand is based on the *marginal revenue product* of labor.

Marginal Revenue Product of Labor (MPR) = the change in a firm's total revenue resulting from the employment of one additional worker. It can also be measured by the marginal physical product of labor multiplied by the price of the good being produced.

$$MRP = \Delta TR / (\Delta Q_L)$$
(where TR is the firm's total revenue and Q_L is the quantity of labor employed)

or…

$$MP_L \times P_G$$
(where MPL is the marginal product of labor and P_G is the price of the good)

MRP is the revenue attributable to the last worker hired… Due to diminishing marginal returns, as more and more workers are hired in the short-run, MRP will decrease, because:
- Labor productivity decreases as labor is added to fixed capital, and in the case of a price-making firm,
- The price of the output must decrease as output increases in order for the firm to sell additional units.

Marginal Revenue Product for a Perfectly Competitive Seller
The marginal revenue product of labor is determined by the productivity of labor and the price of the output. Consider the production data for a bakery below.
- The bakery sells its bread in a perfectly competitive market at a price of $2 per loaf
- The bakery can hire anywhere from 1 to 8 workers.
- Calculating the MRP will tell the bakery how much revenue each additional worker adds to the firm's total revenue.

Quantity of labor (Q_L)	Total Product per hour (TP)	Marginal Product per hour (MP)	Price of the Product (P)	Marginal Revenue Product (MPxP)
0	0	-	-	
1	6	6	2	12
2	11	5	2	10
3	15	4	2	8
4	18	3	2	6
5	20	2	2	4
6	21	1	2	2
7	21	0	2	0
8	20	-1	2	-2

Calculate the MRP of each worker:
- Multiply the marginal product of each worker (how much output she contributes) and the price of bread.

- This tells us *the most the bakery would be willing to pay each worker,* or, the DEMAND FOR LABOR

The MRP of labor is analogous with the firm's demand for labor. This is because:
- MRP tells the firm how much additional revenue each worker adds to the total revenue
- The firm will be willing to pay anything UP TO, but not greater than, each worker's MRP in order to hire that worker.

Quantity of labor (Q_L)	Marginal Revenue Product $(MP_L \times P_G)$
0	–
1	12
2	10
3	8
4	6
5	4
6	2
7	0
8	-2

Consider, for example, the 4th worker in the bakery:
- The fourth worker contributed 3 additional loaves of bread per hour to the bakery's output
- Each loaf sold for $2
- So the worker was accountable for $6 per hour of additional revenue for the bakery.
- The bakery would happily pay this worker $3 per hour, or even $4, or ever $5, or even $5.99!

The bakery would be willing to pay the baker up to, but no more than $6 per hour, since this is exactly how much revenue the worker contributes per hour!

By plotting the marginal revenue product of labor against the

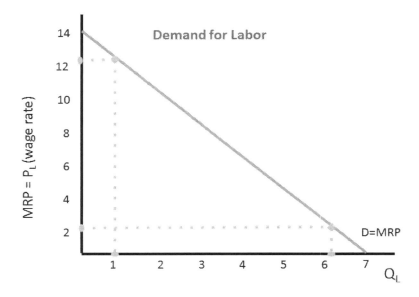

quantity of labor hired, we can see the firm's demand for labor curve.

Notice from the graph:
- There is clearly an inverse relationship between the quantity of labor demanded and the wage rate.
- At higher wage rates, a lower number of workers will be hired (because the MRP has to be high enough to cover the wages paid)
- At lower wage rates a larger number of workers is demanded (since the firm can afford to hire workers with a lower MRP).

Marginal Revenue Product for an Imperfectly Competitive Seller
Now let's consider how the level of competition in the product market will affect a firm's demand for labor. Assume now that our bakery is selling bread in an imperfectly competitive market, making the firm a *price-maker*. The bakery must now lower its price to sell additional loaves of bread.

Quantity of labor (Q_L)	Total Product per hour (TP)	Marginal Product per hour (MP_L)	Price of the Good (P_G)	Marginal Revenue Product (MP_L x P)
0	0	-	-	
1	6	6	5	30
2	11	5	4	20
3	15	4	3	12
4	18	3	2	6
5	20	2	1	2
6	21	1	0.8	0.8
7	21	0	0.8	0
8	20	-1	1	-1

Calculate the MRP of each worker:
- Notice that now BOTH marginal product AND the price of bread falls,
- The bakery is willing to pay more for the first couple workers, because the price of bread is high
- But MRP falls more rapidly than it did for the perfectly competitive seller.

An imperfectly competitive seller's demand for labor will be much less responsive to changes in the wage rate than a perfectly competitive seller. In other words, demand for labor is more *inelastic* among monopolistic firms (and other imperfectly competitive sellers).

Quantity of labor (Q$_L$)	Marginal Revenue Product (MPxP)
0	-
1	30
2	20
3	12
4	6
5	2
6	0.8
7	0
8	-1

Demand for labor is highly inelastic:
- To go from one worker to 2 workers, the seller would require a $10 decrease in the wage rate. This compares to the perfectly competitive seller, which hired a second worker when the wage fell by only $2
- Because the price of bread decreases as the bakery makes more bread, it is very hesitant to hire additional workers, i.e. demand for labor is *wage inelastic*

By plotting the marginal revenue product of labor against the quantity of labor hired, we can see the firm's demand for labor curve.

Notice from the graph:
- The upper line represents the imperfectly competitive seller's demand for labor.
- The lower line is the perfectly competitive seller's demand for labor
- The imperfectly competitive seller's labor demand begins at a higher wage rate (since it can sell bread at a higher price at first), but drops rapidly with the additional workers hired due to the fact that both MP and P are

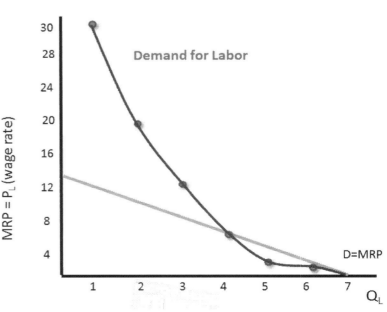

declining as output increases.

Competitive Labor Markets – Market Demand for Labor
The demand for labor is based on the marginal revenue product of labor in a particular industry.
- Above we showed an individual firms' demand for labor.
- In the labor market as a whole, demand for labor consists of the sum of all the individual firms in the market.

Assume, for example, that there are 100 bakeries competing to hire bakers. Each firm has the MRP for labor that we calculated previously. *Market labor demand is simply the sum of all the individual firms competing for workers.*

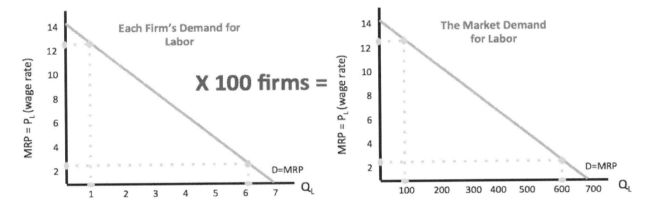

Competitive Labor Markets – Market Supply of Labor
To understand how supply of labor is determined, we must only imagine how households respond to changes in the wage rate being paid to a particular type of worker:

There is a direct relationship between the wage rate and the supply of labor
- Imagine the wages for bakers is rising. More individuals will be willing and able to become bakers at higher wage rates, since it means more income is to be earned!
- If wages for bakers are falling, fewer individuals will be willing and able to work as bakers, since it would mean lower income for the households.

The equilibrium wage rate and the quantity of labor employed in a perfectly competitive labor market is determined by the intersection of labor supply and labor demand!

Marginal Resource Cost
A firm faces a downward sloping demand for labor curve due to the decreasing productivity of labor in the short-run (and for a price-maker, the

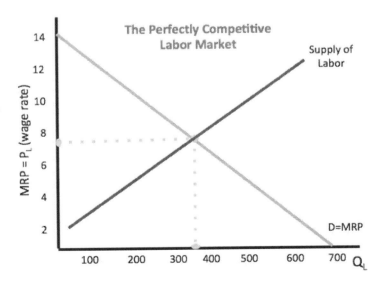

falling prices of its output). To determine exactly how many workers a firm should hire, it must consider not only the MRP of labor, but also the Marginal Resource Cost:

Marginal Resource Cost (MRC): The cost to a firm of hiring one additional worker.

$$MRC = \Delta TC / \Delta Q_L$$
(where TC is the firm's total cost and Q_L is the quantity of labor employed)

In perfectly competitive labor markets, MRC = the Wage Rate: A "wage-taker" is a firm that can hire as many workers as it wants at the market wage rate. The cost of each additional worker, therefore, is simply the wage the firm must pay that worker, which never changes as the level of employment changes!

In a monopsonistic labor market, MRC is always greater than the wage rate: A "wage-maker" is a firm that must raise the wages it offers workers in order to attract more individuals to come work for the firm. Since hiring one more worker requires raising wages for workers who are already employed, the cost of hiring the additional worker is higher than the actual wage the firm has to pay that worker.

Profit Maximization Rule of Resource Employment
Based on what we know about MRP (the change in a firm's revenues of hiring one more worker) and MRC (the change in a firm's costs of hiring one more worker), the decision of how many workers to employ can be thought of as simple *cost/benefit analysis.*

The Profit Maximization Rule of Resource Employment: If the cost of hiring an additional worker (the MRC) is less than the benefit of hiring the worker (the MRP), then the worker should be hired! If the cost is greater than the benefit, then he should not be hired.

Workers should be hired up until the MRP = MRC

In perfectly competitive labor markets, this means individual firms should hire workers until the MRP of the last worker is equal to the market wage rate.

Profit Maximization in a Perfectly Competitive Labor Market
Based on this rule, a perfectly competitive employer will want to hire workers until the MRP of the last worker equals the market wage rate.

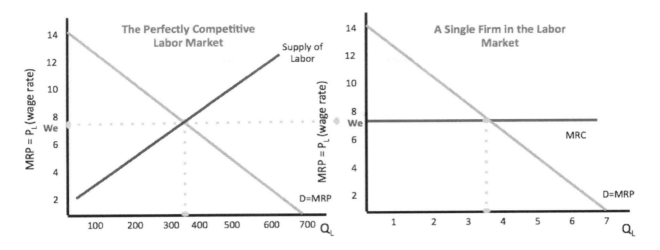

The MRC seen by the individual firm is the market wage rate (We). The "wage-taker" can hire as many workers as it wishes at We.

Profit Maximization in a Monopsonistic Labor Market

As explained previously, a monopsonist is a firm that must raise wages to attract new workers to the market. The firm is a "wage-maker". For this reason, the MRC is always going to be greater than the wage rate the firm is actually paying.

Observe from the graph:

- Because the single employer must raise wages to attract more workers, it will always cost the firm more to hire one more worker than the wage it has to pay that worker.
- Wages must be raised for all workers!
- The MRC rises faster than the wage rate.
- As a result, the firm will hire fewer workers and pay them lower wages than would be paid in a perfectly competitive labor market!

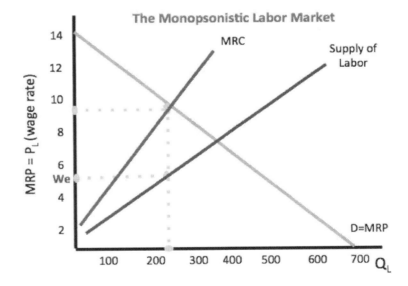

135

Employment in Perfectly Competitive vs. Monopsonistic Markets

Due to its wage-making ability, a monopsonist will employ fewer workers and pay lower wages than would be hired in a perfectly competitive labor market.

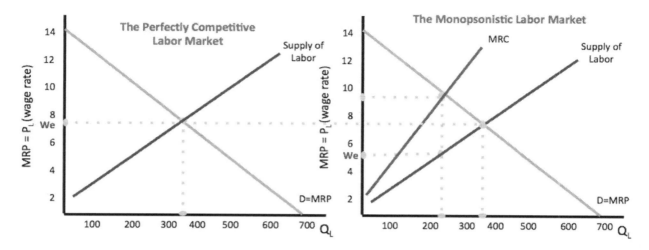

Monopsonistic labor markets are undesirable to workers, for whom there will be fewer employment opportunities and lower wages offered.

Minimum Wages in Labor Markets

Assume the government sets a minimum wage in the two labor markets below. A *minimum wage* is a price floor in a labor market, set above the equilibrium wage rate.

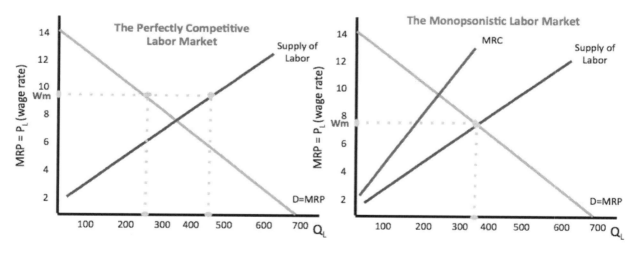

The minimum wage has different effects on a labor market based on the degree of competitiveness in the market. Observe the following:

In the perfectly competitive labor market: *A minimum wage increases unemployment*
- The minimum wage is higher than the equilibrium wage rate.
- The quantity of labor supplied increases as more working age individuals will seek employment due to the government-guaranteed wage.

- The quantity demanded of labor decreases as firms will be less willing to pay the higher wage imposed by the government.
- The result is a *disequilibrium* in the labor market, where Qs>Qd. This translates to unemployment, as there are more job seekers than there are jobs.

In the monopsonistic labor market: *A minimum wage increases employment*
- Before the minimum wage, the single employer faced an MRC that was always higher than the wage it had to pay to hire additional workers.
- This restricted the level of employment the firm desired to the MRC=MRP level.
- With the minimum wage, the firm can hire as many workers as it wants at Wm. The minimum wage *becomes* the marginal resource cost. The firm is now a *wage-taker*.
- As a result, the firm will actually hire MORE workers than it did when it was a *wage maker*.
- The result is a new equilibrium level of employment that is *greater than* before the minimum wage was imposed.

Conclusion: A minimum wage may have negative unintended consequences when labor markets are highly competitive, in the form of higher unemployment (while those who remain employed receive higher wages). However, in monopsonistic labor markets, the imposition of a minimum wage may lead to greater employment and higher wages for those employed.

The Least Cost Combination of Resource Employment
When deciding on the optimal combination of two resources (say workers and robots) a firm should consider the *marginal product per dollar spent* on each resource.
- Similar to the utility maximization rule of consumer behavior, which said that consumers should buy the goods that provide them with the most marginal utility per dollar.
- When a firm employs the resource that gives it the most marginal product per dollar, the firm is maximizing its "bang for its buck"

The Least Cost Combination of Resources: When a firm is hiring two resources (labor and capital) it should attempt to employ them up to the point where the last dollar spent on labor yielded the same additional output as the last dollar spent on capital:

$$MP_L/P_L = MP_C/P_C$$

Where... MP_L is the marginal product of labor and P_L is the price of labor, and
MP_C is the marginal product of capital and P_c is the price of capital

Microeconomics Glossary

Ad valorem taxes	Indirect taxes which are a percentage of the price of the good. For example a 20% alcohol tax would be $2 on a $10 bottle of wine but $4 on a $20 bottle of wine.
Allocative efficiency	When the firms in a market produce the level of output that society demands. If the marginal benefit enjoyed by consumers equals the marginal cost faced by producers, allocative efficiency is achieved. Only in perfect competition will allocative efficiency be achieved in the long-run, since the price of the good equals the marginal cost of the producers. In imperfectly competitive markets, the price will always be higher than the marginal cost of the firms, indicating that resources are under-allocated towards the product.
Asymmetric Information	When one party in an economic transaction knows information pertinent to the transaction that he or she withholds from the other party in an attempt to get a better deal for him or herself. For example, if a used car dealer knows that a car he's selling has been in an accident, but does not reveal this to the buyer. Asymmetric information is a source of market failure, since in some markets resources will be mis-allocated due to asymmetric information.
Average Fixed Cost (AFC)	The total fixed costs (of land and capital) of a particular level of output divided by the quantity being produced.
Average total cost	The total cost of a particular level of output divided by the quantity produced. Equals the average variable cost plus the average fixed cost.
Average variable cost	The total variable costs (of labor and raw materials) of a particular level of output divided by the quantity being produced.
Barriers to entry	The factors which make it costly or difficult for a firm to begin producing a particular good. Might include high start-up costs, legal barriers such as patents and government licenses, or ownership of the factors of production.
Black market	Informal, unofficial markets in which goods are exchanged free of government control. Black market sometimes emerge if price controls exist in the formal market for the good. For example, if the government sets a price ceiling on gasoline, shortages will arise and it may become available on a black market for a price higher than that allowed by the government.
Break-even price	When a firm produces at a price and quantity combination at which the price equals the firm's average total cost of production. The firm covers all of its explicit and implicit costs and thus earns a normal profit, but no economic profit. The firm's total revenue equals its total costs. No economic profits are losses are being earned.

Buffer stock systems	A system of price controls used in a nation by which the government intervenes to keep the price above a minimum and below a maximum. Usually used in markets for agricultural commodities that can be stored for long periods of time. If the market price falls below a minimum level, the government will come in to buy up any surpluses, which get put into storage. If the price rises above a maximum level, the government will release its buffer stocks to keep the price low. Meant to assure stable prices to farmers and consumers of key food commodities.
Capital	Human-made resources (machinery and equipment) used to produce goods and services; goods that do not directly satisfy human wants.
Cartel	When oligopolistic sellers agree to act together to restrict output and raise the price, essentially producing at the monopoly level of output.
Ceteris paribus	"All else equal"; used as a reminder that all variables other than the ones being studied are assumed to be constant.
Choice	In economics, decisions must be made between the various alternative uses for society's scarce resources. Every choice involves an opportunity cost.
Circular flow	A model of the macro economy that shows the interconnectedness of businesses, households, government, banks and the foreign sectors in resource markets and product markets. Money flows in a circular direction, and goods, services and resources flow in the opposite direction.
Collusion	When oligopolistic sellers cooperate on output and price, allowing for a more optimal payoff (profit) that would be achieved under competition.
Command Economy	An economic system in which resources are allocated through central planning, usually by the state or central government.
Commodity	A good widely demanded (often globally) and supplied by many sellers, usually without much product differentiation between sellers. Commodities are standardized products. The price of commodities is determined by the market as a whole, often in the global market, not by any individual producer or group of producers. Often traded on national or international commodities markets. Examples include oil, wheat, corn, coffee, copper, cotton, tin, rice, gold, and other primary goods.
Common access resources	Natural resources over which there is no established private ownership. They are owned by no one, thus available to anyone to use. Their existence gives rise to the tragedy of the commons.
Complements	Goods that are used in conjunction with one another. They are typically consumed together. For example hamburgers and French fries.

Consumer Surplus	The additional benefit enjoyed by consumers who are willing to pay more for a product than the market price. Graphically it is the area of the triangle below the demand curve and above the equilibrium price, out to the equilibrium quantity.
Contestable markets	A monopolistically competitive market in which economic profits are being earned. Barriers to entry are relatively low and new firms may enter the market to grab profits, and easily leave once no more profits can be earned.
Corrective subsidy	A payment from the government to the producers or consumers of a merit good, or one that creates positive externalities in its production or consumption. Meant to achieve a more socially optimal level of output.
Corrective tax (Pigouvian tax)	A tax on the production of a demerit good, or one that creates negative externalities in its production or consumption. Meant to achieve a more socially optimal level of output.
Cross-price Elasticity of demand (XED)	A measure of the responsiveness of consumers of one good to changes in the price of a related good (either a complement or a substitute). Calculated as the percentage change in the quantity of Good A divided by the percentage change in the price of Good B. Can be negative (for complementary goods) or positive (for substitute goods).
Deadweight loss	(Welfare loss): The loss of total societal welfare (consumer and produce surplus) that occurs when a market is producing at a level of output that is not socially optimal (where MSB=MSC). May arise from a market failure or from a government intervention in an already efficient market.
Demand	A schedule or curve showing the quantities of a particular good demanded at a range of price in a particular period of time.
Depreciation (microeconomics)	The decrease in the value of factors of production over time. Capital depreciates as it becomes more expensive to maintain over time.
Derived Demand	When the demand for something depends on the demand for something else. For example the demand for oil depends on the demand for gasoline, which is the finished product that oil is used to produce.
Diamond and Water Paradox	Water, which is demanded by everyone, is extremely cheap. But diamonds, who are demanded only by the very few, are incredibly expensive. The paradox is, "how can something for which there is so little demand be so expensive?" The solution to this riddle is that the value of something is based not only on the demand for it, but also on its supply. Scarcity, in other words, is a function of both supply and demand. Diamonds are incredibly expensive because, despite their limited demand, their supply is so extremely limited that they are deemed to have great value. Water, despite its high demand, is in such abundant supply that it is very cheap.

Differentiation	When firms attempt to set their products apart from the competition through improvements in technology, branding, service, location and other means. The goal is to increase demand for the individual firm's product at the expense of the competition, giving the firm more price marking power and allowing for economic profits to be earned.
Diminishing marginal returns	The principle that says as more of a variable resource (usually labor) is added to fixed resources (land and capital), the output attributable to additional units of the variable resource declines as more and more is added. Explained by the fact that in order for workers to remain productive as more workers are hired, more capital is needed. Without more capital, productivity declines as labor is added to production.
Diminishing marginal utility	One of the explanations for the law of demand and the downward sloping demand curve. Says that the more of any particular product consumers have, the less each additional unit is worth to them. In other words, the less scarce a particular product, the lower its value in the market. An example might be the iPhone, which when it came out was very scarce (in high demand but limited supply). Apple charged very high prices for the first iPhones. But as the product has become more widely available, each additional iPhone Apple makes is harder and harder to sell. It therefore must come out with new versions of the iPhone every year that are different from previous versions to keep demand strong.
Diseconomies of scale	When a firm gets "too big for its own good". If a firm expands beyond a certain size, it begins experiencing inefficiencies that cause its average costs to rise as output increases.
Disequilibrium	When the price in a market is either too high or too low, so that the quantities supplied and demanded are not the same. If a price is higher than equilibrium, there will be a surplus in the market, meaning the quantity supplied will be greater than the quantity demanded. If a price is below equilibrium, there will be a shortage, meaning that the quantity demanded will be greater than the quantity supplied.
Economic good	Something that is demanded and limited in quantity, thus scarce.
Economic profit	Also called "abnormal" profit. This is the revenues earned by a firm beyond that which is needed to cover all explicit costs (wages, rent and interest) and what the business owner expects to earn (normal profit). Entrepreneurs are attracted to industries in which economic profits can be earned.
Economic resources	Land, labor, capital, and entrepreneurial ability, which are used in the production of goods and services. They are economic resources because they are scarce (limited in supply and desired). Also called the factors of production.

Economies of Scale	"The benefits of being big." As a firm increases its output in the long run, it adds more factories, acquires more capital and land and labor and sees its average total costs decrease as it grows. This arises due to factors such as increase efficiency, bulk-ordering, reduced shipping costs, increased bargaining power with resource suppliers and labor unions, more favorable interest rates from lenders, etc…
Elastic Demand	When consumers are relatively responsive to price changes. A PED coefficient of more than one means that a particular change in the price of a good will be met by a proportionally larger change in the quantity demanded.
Entrepreneurship	The creativity and innovation an individual business owner puts towards the production of goods and services.
Equilibrium	Refers to the price and quantity determined in a market when the supply equals the demand. At equilibrium there are no surpluses or shortages of the product; at the equilibrium price the quantity supplied equals the quantity demanded.
Externalities	When the production or consumption of a good creates either positive or negative effects on a third party not involved in the goods production or consumption. Can be negative (spillover costs) or positive (spillover benefits)
Factors of Production	Include the human and natural resource needed to produce any good or service: Land, labor, capital and entrepreneurship
Fixed Costs	Costs that do not change with the level of output in the short-run. Fixed costs must be paid regardless of the level of output. For example rental payment and interest payments on a bakery remain the same regardless of whether the bakery makes 10 muffins or 10,000 muffins. These costs are fixed.
Flat rate taxes	Indirect taxes which are of a fixed amount, rather than a percentage of the sales price. For example a $3 per pack tax on cigarettes. It would be $3 whether the sales price is $2 or $5.
Free good	A good that is demanded, but not limited in quantity, thus it is not scarce. Air is an example.
Free market economy	An economic system in which resources are allocated purely by the forces of demand, supply and the price mechanism. The government has no influence over what is produced, how it is produced and for whom.
Free Trade	The exchange of goods and services between different countries undertaken without any government intervention.

Giffen Goods	Goods for which the quantity demanded increases as the price increases. Usually they are inferior goods that when the price rises, low-income consumers of the good feel poorer since their disposable incomes fall. Due to the fact that they feel poorer, consumers end up buying more of the inferior good whose price rose. Mostly a theoretical exception to the law of demand.
Goods	The physical output of a firm producing a product meant for sale and consumption in a product market. Contrast with services, which are non-physical products produced and sold by firms to consumers.
Homogenous	Means "identical". The output of a perfectly competitive firm is homogeneous to all other firms in the market.
Incentive	Refers to the motivation an individual has to undertake a particular action.
Income	The money earned by households for providing their resources (land, labor and capital) to firms in the resource market. Incomes include wages, interest, rent and profit.
Income effect	One explanation for the law of demand. Says that as the price of a good decreases, consumers feel as if they have more disposable income, thus tend to consumer more of the good whose price is falling. On the other hand, as the price of a good rise, real income decreases, consumers feel poorer, thus consume less of the good.
Income Elasticity of Demand (YED)	A measure of the responsiveness of consumers of a particular good to changes in their income. Calculated as the percentage change in the quantity of a good divided by the percentage change in consumers' income. Can be negative (inferior goods) or positive (normal goods).
Indirect Taxation	Taxes placed on consumption. Considered indirect because households only pay them when they buy a good, compared to a direct tax on their income.
Inelastic Demand	When consumers are relatively unresponsive to price changes. A PED coefficient of less than one means that a particular change in the price of a good will be met by a proportionally smaller change in the quantity demanded.
Inferior Goods	Goods that consumers demand less of as their incomes rise and more of as their incomes fall. For example fast food meals.
Interdependence	When the level of profit of one firm in a market depends not only on that firm's decisions regarding output and price but also on the decisions of the small number of other competitors in the market.
Interest	The payment for capital in the resource market. Firms pay interest on the money they borrow to acquire capital equipment (technology). Households receive interest for providing their savings to banks, which make the loans to the firms paying interest.

Interest rate	The opportunity cost of money. Either the cost of borrowing money or the cost of spending money. What would be given up by not saving money.
Investment	A component of aggregate demand, it includes all spending on capital equipment, inventories, and technology by firms. This does not include financial investment, which is the purchase of financial assets (stocks and bonds), not included in GDP because they are only purely financial investments.
Labor	The work undertaken by humans towards the production of goods and services
Land	Includes all natural resources needed to undertake production of goods or services: including soil, timber, minerals, fossil fuels, fresh water, livestock, fish, etc... "the gifts of nature"
Law of Demand	Ceteris paribus, there is an inverse relationship between the price of a good and the quantity demanded by consumers. At higher prices, less of a particular good tends to be demanded, while at lower prices, more of a good tends to be demanded. Can be explained by the income effect, the substitution effect and the law of diminishing marginal utility.
Law of increasing opportunity cost	As more of a particular product is produced, the opportunity cost in terms of what must be given up of other goods increases. Explains the convex shape of a nation's production possibilities curve.
Law of Supply	Ceteris paribus, there exists a direct relationship between the price of a good and the quantity supplied by producers. Explains why the supply curve slopes upwards. As the price of good rises, sellers wish to supply greater quantities as the possibility for economic profits is greater. At lower prices, less output is produced since it is harder to earn profits. Firms are profit seekers.
Lump sum tax	A one-time payment from producers to the government. Contrasts with a per unit tax, which is levied on every unit of output produced, thus increases in size as output increases. A lump sum tax increases firms' average fixed cost, and thus average total cost, but has no effect on marginal cost or average variable cost.
Marginal	Means "additional". An important term in economics, which often focuses on "marginal analysis" meaning we compare the additional cost of an action to the additional benefit it creates.
Marginal analysis	Decision making which involves a comparison of marginal (extra) benefits and marginal costs.
Marginal Cost	The change in total costs resulting from an increase in output by one unit in the short run.
Marginal Private Benefit (MPB)	The benefits enjoyed by the individual consumers of a particular good. Does not take into account any external benefits or costs arising from a goods consumption.

Marginal Private Cost (MPC)	The private cost of an additional unit of output of a good experienced by an individual firm. Does takes into account only the explicit and implicit costs faced by the firm, and does not include external costs (the social or environmental costs which may arise from the production of a good).
Marginal Product	The change in the total product resulting from the addition of one worker in the short run.
Marginal Revenue	The change in a firm's total revenue resulting from one additional unit of output
Marginal Social Benefit (MSB)	The benefits experienced by the individual consumers of a particular good, plus or minus any social or environmental benefits or costs. MSB can be greater than marginal private benefit (MPB) if there are positive externalities of consumption (e.g. education) or less than MPB if there are negative externalities of consumption (e.g. smoking).
Marginal Social Cost (MSC)	The private costs faced by producers of a particular good plus any external costs placed on third parties, such as environmental or social costs, arising from a good's production.
Market	A place where buyers and sellers meat to engage in mutual trade. Prices are set by the interaction of demand and supply in a market.
Market Failure	When the free market fails to achieve a socially optimal allocation of resources towards the production of a particular good or service.
Market system	Market economic system: A system of resource allocation in which buyers and sellers meet in markets to determine the price and quantity of goods, services and productive resources.
Merit goods	Products that create positive externalities, or spillover benefits, on a third party due to their production and/or consumption. For example, vaccines are a merit good since they make all of society healthier, not just the individual who receives them.
Microeconomics	The study of the interactions between consumers and producers in markets for individual products.
Money	Any object that can be used to facilitate the exchange of goods and services in a market.
Monopolistic Competition	Monopolistic Competition A market in which a relatively large number of firms competes with one another by differentiating their products from the competition. Economic profits can be earned in the short-run through successful product differentiation, but due to the low barriers to entry they are unlikely in the long-run. Monopolistic competition is the most common market structure, and included restaurants, automobiles, clothes, salons, etc...

Monopoly	A market in which only one firm produces all the output. A monopolist is a single seller, protected by high entry barriers, producing a unique product with the ability to set the price and level of output based on its own profit-maximizing decisions.
Natural Monopoly	A market in which the demand for the product intersects the single firm's average total cost curve while it is still downward sloping. In other words, there is not enough demand to warrant more than one firm producing the good. Society is actually better off with a single producer. Examples include utilities such as electricity and water. Often natural monopolies are regulated by government to assure a more socially optimal level of output and price.
Normal Good	Goods that consumers demand more of as their incomes rise and less of as their incomes fall. For example restaurant meals.
Normal Profit	The implicit cost faced by the owner of a business firm. A business owner will wish to cover all of his explicit costs (wages, rents and interest payment), but also earn a "normal" level of profit in order to remain in a market in the long run. If the entrepreneur does not enjoy a normal level of profit, he will shut down his business and re-allocated his resources into another industry in which a higher level of profit can be earned. Normal profit is a cost, because if it is not earned, a firm will eventually shut down.
Normative statement	A normative statement is one based on opinion. For example, "the government should lower income taxes".
Oligopoly	A market in which a relatively small number of firms compete with one another in a strategic manner. Characterized by a strong interdependence between the small number of firms. Barriers to entry are high and firms are hesitant to change their prices due to the fact that price wars may result when prices are lowered, and significant market share can be lost if prices are raised. Such markets tend to be highly inefficient due to the lack of competition.
Opportunity cost	What must be given up to have anything else. Not necessarily monetary costs, rather include what you could do with the resources you use to undertake any activity or exchange.
Per unit tax	A tax levied on producers for every unit produced. In contrast to a lump sum tax, which is a one time payment from producers to the government. A per unit tax increases firm's marginal cost and average variable cost (thus, also the average total cost), but does not affect fixed costs. A per unit tax will likely cause a firm to reduce its output in the short-run, since MC shifts up and moves along the demand curve.
Perfect Competition	A market structure in which a very large number of firms compete to sell a homogeneous product. There are no barriers to entry or exit, no firm is able to charge a price higher than any other firm, and in the long-run no economic profits or the firms in the market will earn losses.

Perfectly elastic Demand	When any change in the price of a good leads to a nearly infinite change in the quantity consumers demand. For example if the price rises at all, no one will wish to buy the good. If the price decreases at all, every consumer will wish to buy the good. Demand for a perfect competitor's output is perfectly elastic, due to the countless perfect substitutes available to consumers.
Perfectly inelastic Demand	When the quantity demanded for a good does not change even as the price rises or falls.
Positive statement	A claim that can be proven with facts. For example, "The unemployment rate has risen for two consecutive quarters."
Potential output	How much a nation can produce if all of its resources (land, labor and capital) are operating at their full capacity and at full efficiency. Contrasts with full employment output, which a nation achieves when most of its resources are employed towards production, but there exist some degree of unemployment (the natural rate of unemployment).
Price	This is the amount paid for a good determined by the supply and demand for the good in the market. Price rises and falls as demand and supply rise and fall.
Price ceiling	A maximum price set by the government, usually below the equilibrium price, meant to lower the price consumers have to pay for a product. An effective price ceiling leads to disequilibrium in the market in which the quantity demanded is greater than the quantity supplied (shortage).
Price discrimination	The practice of a firm charging different prices to different consumers for an identical product. Only possible if the firm can a) segregate the market between consumers with different elasticities of demand, and b) prevent resale of the good.
Price Elasticity of Demand (PED)	A measure of the responsiveness of consumers to a change in the price of a particular good. Measures the percent change in quantity divided by the percentage change in the price of a good.
Price Elasticity of Supply (PES)	A measure of the responsiveness of producers to changes in the price of a good. Calculated as the percentage change in the quantity supplied divided by the percentage change in the price.
Price floor	A minimum price set by the government, usually above the equilibrium price, meant to increase the price that producers receive for their output. An effective price floor leads to a disequilibrium in the market in which the quantity supplied is greater than the quantity demanded (surplus)
Price mechanism	Determines the allocation of resources between society's competing wants and needs in a free market system. Prices act as signals from buyers to sellers as to what is most demanded by society.

Producer surplus	The additional benefit enjoyed by producers who would have been willing to sell their product for less than the market price. Graphically it is the area of the triangle below the equilibrium price and above the supply curve, out to the equilibrium quantity.
Product market	The market in a nation's circular flow of income in which households demand goods and services, which firms provide. Households make purchases, providing revenue for firms, which they in turn use to acquire resources from households in the resource market.
Production possibilities curve	A graph that shows the various combinations of output that the economy can possibly produce given the available factors of production and the available production technology.
Productive efficiency	When a good is produces in the least cost manner, productive efficiency is achieved. This means that firms producing the good are achieving the lowest possible average production cost; in other words, they are producing at the lowest point on their average total cost curve, where marginal cost intersects the ATC. Among the four market structures (perfect competition, monopolistic competition, oligopoly and monopoly), only perfectly competitive firms will achieve productive efficiency in the long-run, since the price in the market will always be competed down to the firms' minimum ATC.
Productivity	The output per unit of input of a resource. An important determinant of the level of aggregate supply in a nation. Will increase as a result of better or more capital, education and health, all which add to the human capital of a nation.
Profit	The payment to the entrepreneur in the resource market. A business owner expects to earn a "normal" level of profit, otherwise it will not be worth his while to remain in a market. In this regard, profit is a cost of production, because if a minimum profit is not earned a firm will shut down.
Profit maximization	When firms produce at the quantity of output at which their total economic profits are at their greatest (or their economic losses are at their lowest). The profit maximizing level of output occurs where a firm's marginal revenue equals its marginal cost.
Public good	Goods or services that are non-excludable by the producers and non-rivalrous in consumption. Because of these characteristics, private sector firms have little or no incentive to produce them, since they would be impossible to sell. Therefore, government must provide public goods. Examples include street lamps, sidewalks and national defense.
Quantity	This is the amount of output produced and consumed in a market determined by the supply and demand. As supply and demand change, the quantity in the market changes as well.

Rationing	Refers to the system by which society's scarce output is allocated between the various groups in society who desire it. The "market system" is one way to ration output, while the "centrally planned" system is another.
Rent	The price of land resources. Rent must be paid by producers, either as an explicit cost or as an opportunity cost for those who own the land resources employed in production.
Resource market	The market in a nation's circular flow in which households provide firms with the factors of production (land, labor and capital) in exchange for money incomes (rent, wages and interest). Firms are the buyers, households are the sellers in the resource market.
Scarcity	When something is both desired and limited in supply. All resources (land, labor and capital) are limited in supply, yet desired for their use in the production of goods and services.
Services	The non-physical output of firms meant for consumption in a product market. Services are "non-tangible" goods, such as taxi rides, accounting, doctor visits, teaching, and other products that can be bought and sold, but not physically consumed.
Shift	Refers to movements of curves in an economic diagram either inward or outward, up or down.
Short-run	(In microeconomics): The period of time over which the amount of land and capital employed in the production of a good is fixed in quantity. "The fixed-plant period". Labor and raw materials are the only variable resources in the short run.
Shortage	When the quantity demanded for a particular good is greater than the quantity supplied. Also called "excess demand". Occurs when the price is below the equilibrium level, for example, when a government imposes a price ceiling in a market.
Shut-down price	If the price of a good falls below a firm's minimum average variable cost, there is no way the firm can hope to cover its labor costs in the short-run, thus the firm must shut down.
Shut-down rule	If a firm experiences economic losses in the short-run which exceeds the firm's total fixed costs, then the firm can minimize its losses by shutting down
Social science	One of the fields of study that examine humans' social interactions and institutions. Includes economics, sociology, psychology, archaeology, political science, linguistics, etc
Socially optimal output	When output occurs at the intersection of marginal social benefit (MSB) and marginal social cost (MSC), the socially optimal level of output is achieved. Also known as the allocatively efficient level of output. If output occurs at any other level, a market failure exists.

Specialization	The practice of allocating an individual's, an organization's or a nation's resources towards the production of a good or a category of goods for which it has a relatively low opportunity cost. Improves the overall allocation of resources and allows individuals and, with trade, allows individuals or nations to consume beyond what they would be able to produce on their own.
Subsidy	Payments made from the government to individuals or firms for the production or consumption of particular goods or services. Subsidies reduce the cost of production or increase the benefit of consumption, and therefore lead to a greater equilibrium quantity in the market for the subsidized good.
Substitute	When a good can be used instead of another good, the two goods are substitutes. For instance, Coke and Pepsi are substitutes. The demand for one good is directly related to the price of its substitutes.
Substitution effect	One of the explanations for the law of demand and the downward sloping demand curve. Says that as the price of a good decreases, it makes substitutes appear more expensive, thus consumers demand more of the now cheaper good. On the other hand, as the price of a good increases, its substitutes appear cheaper and consumers will switch to alternative products.
Supply	A schedule or curve showing the direct relationship between the quantity of output firms produce in a particular period of time and the various prices of the good.
Supply shock	Anything that leads to a sudden, unexpected change in a good's supply. Can be negative (decreases supply) or positive (increases supply). May result from a change in energy prices, wages, business taxes, or may result from a natural disaster or a new discovery of important resources.
Surplus	When the quantity supplied of a good is greater than the quantity demanded. Also called "excess supply". A surplus will occur if the price in a market is greater than the equilibrium price, for example, due to a government price floor.
Sustainability	The ability to endure over time. Sustainable growth requires that resources are used at a rate at which they are able to replenish themselves and the environment is not despoiled in the process of production.
Tax	A payment made by an individual or a firm to the government, usually levied on income, property or the consumption of goods and services. Taxes are a leakage from the circular flow of income, but they provide government with the money they use to provide government services and public goods.

Tax incidence	(Sometimes called tax burden) When an indirect tax is placed on a particular good or group of goods, the incidence, or burden, of the tax is shared by producers and consumers. Buyers will pay a higher price, thus share some of the burden of the tax. But once the tax has been paid to the government, producers end up keeping a lower price, meaning they also share some of the tax burden. The amount of a tax on a particular good paid by consumers is the consumer tax incidence; the amount paid by producers is the producer tax incidence.
The Basic Economic Questions	What should be produced? How should it be produced? and, "For whom should production take place?" Any economic system, either centrally planned or free market, must address these questions.
Total cost	The total expenditures made by a firm on land, capital, labor and the entrepreneurship of the business owner towards the production of a good or service at a particular level of output.
Total Product	The total output of a firm.
Total Revenue	What a firm earns from the sale of its output. Equals the price of the output multiplied by the quantity sold.
Tradable permits	A market-based solution to correcting negative production externalities. The government issues or sells permits allowing firms to emit a pre-determined quantity of pollution (such as CO_2) into the environment. If a producer wishes to exceed the amount they are permitted, they must purchase additional permits from other firms. Firms that reduce their emissions may sell permits they no longer require, adding to the firm's revenues. Dirty firms end up paying more to produce, while greener firms earn greater revenues from selling permits they no longer require; thereby such a scheme creates a strong incentive to reduce pollution.
Tragedy of the commons	When there exists a common access resource, over which there is no private owner, the incentive among rational users of that resource is to exploit it to the fullest potential in order to maximize their own self gain before the resource is depleted. The tragedy, therefore, is that common resources will inevitably be depleted due to humans' self-interested behavior, leaving us with shortages in key resources essential to human survival.
Transfer payments	Payments from the government to one group of individuals using tax money raised from taxes on another group of individuals. Meant to reallocate income in an economy, often times from the rich to the poor, but also from households to firms (in the case of subsidies for certain industries).
Unit elastic Demand	When a particular change in the price of a good is met by a proportionally identical change in the quantity demanded. A PED coefficient of 1 indicates unit elastic demand.

Utility Maximization Rule	$MUx/Px = MUy/Py$, where MUx is the marginal utility derived from good x, Px is the price of good x, MUy is the marginal utility of good y and Py is the price of good y. A consumer should spend his limited money income on the goods that give him the most marginal utility per dollar. Only when the ratio of MU/P is equal for all goods is a consumer maximizing his total utility.
Variable Cost	Costs that change with the level of output in the short-run. Typically these are the labor costs and raw material costs a firm faces. To produce more of a good in the short-run, more labor and raw materials are needed, so variable costs increase as output increases.
Veblen good	Ostentatious goods for which the quantity demanded increases as the price rises. Individuals who consume these goods do so only because they are very expensive and therefore a sign of their status and wealth.
Wage	The payment to labor in the resource market. Wages are the "price of labor"
Wealth	An important determinant of consumption. Refers to the total value of a household's assets minus all its liabilities.

35988929R00087

Made in the USA
Lexington, KY
06 October 2014